Don't be Shy

Don't be Shy
How to Beat Shyness and Face the World

Dr Kenneth Hambly

Thorsons
An Imprint of HarperCollins*Publishers*

Thorsons
An Imprint of HarperCollins*Publishers*
77–85 Fulham Palace Road,
Hammersmith, London W6 8JB

Published by Thorsons 1991
10 9 8 7 6 5 4 3 2

A catalogue record for this book
is available from the British Library

ISBN 0 7225 2464 1

Printed in Great Britain by
Woolnough Bookbinding Limited
Irthlingborough, Northamptonshire

Contents

Introduction

We all feel shy on some occasions. We may go to a party and be overawed by the event or by the people present. We feel uncomfortable and conspicuous; we wish we were somewhere else altogether. Everyone knows how that feels, but some people feel like that much of the time. They may be extremely uncomfortable in company, and their shyness may even make it difficult for them to lead normal lives. For them, shyness is a real problem.

If you are one of these people, or if shyness seems to be holding you back, you may wish that there was something you could do to make you less shy. Why can't you be like everyone else, enjoying parties, enjoying meeting people, having boyfriends or girlfriends, being successful in your work and in your social life? Yet no matter how much you wish you were less shy, there seems to be nothing that you can do about it. Shyness seems to be an affliction you are stuck with.

On the other hand, we all know someone who did become less shy. It may be a girl who gets a boyfriend. Her friends notice the difference—she seems to be a new person altogether, full of confidence, enjoying life, her shyness a thing of the past. Or it may be a boy who gets a new job. He is a changed person too. His new responsibility has somehow transformed him and he seems to be less shy and more confident. If it is possible to become less shy through changed circumstances, is there not something we could do for ourselves to make us less shy? Common sense would suggest that there is.

If you are shy and if it is a problem for you, it's time you did something about it. There are things that you can do, and you can overcome shyness if you go about it the right way. It will take a little time and a little effort, but if shyness is making your life even very slightly less comfortable, less pleasant or less successful than it should be, it is worth both time and effort. This book will help you to overcome your shyness using simple techniques which you can use in your everyday life. If you practise them and apply them, you will be more relaxed and more comfortable in most situations, and in the long term your life will be more fulfilled.

So please, don't be shy!

Chapter 1

Shyness—what is it?

We all think that we know what shyness is, but do we really know? It would be difficult to define shyness in a few words. The dictionary tries to do so, but its definition—e.g. easily frightened, timid—seems rather inadequate. Of course if you suffer from shyness, you know exactly what it means, and you know that it is a compelling and perplexing phenomenon which can affect every part of your life. It almost defies definition. It isn't just that you feel awkward and uncomfortable in company. If you suffer from shyness you begin to fear some social situations; you may begin to avoid them, so your lifestyle may become limited.

Shyness is also a problem in that it is common in young people, and is often associated with encounters with members of the opposite sex, so that meeting boys or girls, going on dates and all the business of forming relationships is made so much more difficult. For the shy person it can be an uphill struggle, and shyness can be a blight on a major part of your life. That isn't a minor annoyance, it is a major disability, and it isn't just in the area of forming relationships. It may affect your work, hindering promotion prospects. You may watch less able people being promoted over your head, or you simply may not apply for some posts because you know that your shyness will make the job intolerable or will make it impossible for you to do well in an interview.

Your shyness

Only you know what your shyness means to you. You know what it is like to be shy every day of your life, to start the day knowing that you are shy and knowing that it is going to affect several events which you will have to face during the coming day. You will know how apprehensive you may feel before a party or a meeting, or before going out on a date. Your shyness is always with you, every day of the year.

You will know something else too. You will know that your shyness will sometimes make you feel very uncomfortable. You will get physical sensations in some situations where you feel particularly shy; it is these sensations which make you feel so uncomfortable, and if they are severe they may even make you feel ill. Shyness can be agony, both physical and mental. Perhaps you haven't thought very much about the physical side of shyness, and if it hasn't been brought to your attention it may be that you aren't aware that shyness has a physical side. Yet if you do think about it, you will realize that there are sometimes physical sensations which you experience in a situation where you feel shy, and they can be very severe.

The more you think about shyness, the more complicated it seems to be. There are many facets to being shy. You may ask yourself why it happens, why you, particularly, have been selected as a sufferer, or whether there is anything unusual or odd about you because you are shy. Then there are questions about what other people think about you, about how socially acceptable you are, worries about how you value yourself and how others value you. On top of that there is the physical pain of the shyness itself. You may think that there are more questions than answers, but that isn't the case. Shyness can be understood with a little thought because there is nothing mysterious about it, and when you understand it you can overcome it.

How common is shyness?

You aren't the only shy person in the world. There are no figures relating to the number of shy people, but shyness is a well-known phenomenon even if it isn't easy to define. It is possible to discover how common shyness is by seeing how it is treated in books. In fact there is very little to find in textbooks and medical papers, so you have to turn to works of fiction to see how it is treated there, and how often it is mentioned. If you read the great novels you can see what people's attitudes have been about shyness over the centuries up to the present time.

It is only recently that heroines in literature have been anything but shy. Erica Jong must have been one of the first authors, in her book *Fear of Flying* to have had a sexually aggressive, super-confident female as the central character in a book. In the past women have been portrayed as being demure and diffident, and these qualities have been esteemed. Women, at least, were allowed to be shy!

For men the situation may be slightly different. Men are expected to be macho, and in our time this has almost become a cult. There are few shy male heroes in popular fiction.

You won't find many people in fiction who suffer from shyness to a degree that affects their lives. That is something which our society chooses to ignore, and it has always been so. Heroes and heroines may be demure, but their lives continue without being disturbed too much by their shyness, and there is rarely a description of the dreadful agony which a shy person may experience in a difficult situation. Yet that is real drama, when you are in a room full to overflowing with people who seem to be totally alien, or when you are expected to make a speech, or when there is someone you particularly want to impress. That's when your heart speeds up and you sweat, you feel that you can't swallow, and on a bad day you either feel that you are going to die, or else you wish that you would die.

This is perhaps what makes shyness such a problem for us at the present time. Our society is going through a period when shyness isn't fashionable, for men or for women. We are all meant to be aggressive participants in the consumer economy and shyness isn't acceptable, either in our workplace or in our social life. Social activities, particularly for young people, are all about parties, 'clubbing' and discos. You are meant to get out there and sock it to them, and that isn't easy if you're shy, so there are a lot of pressures on shy people these days.

Your attitudes to your shyness

Every shy person worries about what other people think of him or her, but what is really important is what shy people think about themselves and what attitude they take to their shyness. Do you care what other people think about you, and do you care enough to want to do something about it? Is your shyness an attractive addition to your personality or is it a blight which bothers you every waking hour of your life? What sort of personality would you like to have? Would it be that of James Bond or a super-hero or would you settle for a reduction in your shyness to a level which would make you more competent in your everyday life and more comfortable in your work and in your social life? Would you like to be somebody else altogether, or would you be perfectly happy with the person you are, if only you could reduce the level of your shyness to reasonable proportions? Perhaps it's time we began thinking about our shyness.

Thinking about your shyness

You may well have spent many hours wishing you were less shy, thinking of all the things you could do if you were less shy, the boyfriends or girlfriends you could have and all the achievements you could have made by now if only you were less shy, but have you really spent much time thinking about shyness itself, about what it is and what you could do about it? The chances are that it is something you have taken for granted, accepted as something that you could really do very little about, apart from wishing with all your heart that you didn't have it.

It's time you sat down and thought about your shyness and decided firstly whether you want to do something about it, secondly what you would like to achieve, and only when you have done that, how you intend to go about doing something about it. If your shyness gets in the way of your everyday life, you will certainly want to do something about it, but there's more to it than that. You have to ask yourself if you want to do something about it badly enough to give time and energy to the difficult task of reducing your shyness. Are you that determined? Is your shyness important enough a problem to really want to take it on head first? No one has said that overcoming shyness is easy.

Looking at your life

Before you answer these questions you should take a critical look at your life. You know that you are shy, but how does that shyness affect your life? We know that you are uncomfortable in some situations, and we have decided that you get unpleasant physical symptoms in some very difficult situations, but is there more to it than that? Could it be that your shyness limits your life, that you are avoiding difficult situations and that your life is actually limited by your shyness? It may be that you aren't staying at home and missing out on social opportunities, that you are attending them but not participating *fully* when you do go to a club or a party.

Shyness may be interfering with your life in many ways, and one of those ways may be at an almost microscopic level, so that you seem to participate in all events normally, but you are really holding back, always the onlooker. That would be all right if you were satisfied with that role, but most probably you are not. You would like to be more of a participant, but your shyness keeps you back. You probably haven't noticed how much that happens because you have made do for so long, perhaps even most of your life, but now is the time to take a critical and honest look at your life in all its aspects and honestly assess how much your shyness holds you back.

If you are going to do that, sit down with a piece of paper and a pencil and consider an average day, perhaps a recent day where you had a lot of things to do and which may not have worked to your complete satisfaction. You might like to start a small notebook because there will be quite a lot of things to write down in the course of this book and it might be interesting to have them to hand so that you can refer to them when necessary, or perhaps later if you want to look back on just how severe your shyness has been. Start your notes by considering your average day.

Make a list of the things you had to do, make a list of some of the things you could have done but didn't. Did your shyness affect the way you spent that day? How did your shyness affect the different events of the day in even the smallest way? Were there any embarrassing moments caused by shyness, and were there any times when you felt less than comfortable? Did you avoid any events or situations? Consider all the events, including the least important, because our lives are made up of small events, of conversations, of giving gifts, giving and receiving compliments, asking about the small events in other people's lives, of making friends of both sexes, of entertaining and being entertained. Life is built from small bricks.

It may be that shyness has a greater effect upon your life than you realize. If that is the case, it is time you did something about it, but if you make that decision you have to commit yourself to some quite hard work, because it isn't easy to overcome shyness.

What would you like to achieve?

One thing you cannot do is to change your personality. You cannot simply become someone else, and you almost certainly wouldn't want to do that anyway. You are someone of value, valued by yourself and by others. What you *do* want to do is to liberate yourself from the shackles of shyness and fulfil your potential. You want to be all that you can be, do everything that you want to do, and be comfortable whilst doing it. That isn't too much to ask, and it is worth working for.

It isn't easy thinking about these things, so it is worth looking at the experiences of other people. We don't live in a vacuum, and many other people have problems and experiences very like our own. They don't necessarily talk about their problems to just anyone, but nearly everyone has problems of some sort or another and as I am a general practitioner people do talk to me, and often I can help them by listening, by advising and often by putting their problems into perspective. It can be a surprise and relief to know that you aren't the only one to have the difficulties and fears that have bothered you for so long. I would like to introduce you to a few people who have had problems which may not be all that dissimilar to your own.

Michael

Michael was 18 when he came to see me. He looked like a normal, healthy and able young man, and indeed that is just what he was. In the course of discussing a minor ailment he had, he mentioned a more serious problem, that of excessive shyness. He was aware that many people were shy, and he was aware that they seemed to be able to manage their shyness, but his shyness was ruining his life and no matter how hard he tried, he didn't seem to be able to do anything about it. He was just about at the end of his tether.

His problem with shyness was just what you might guess it to be in a young man of 18. His problem related particularly to young women. He had found that he couldn't talk to girls, couldn't even be in the same room as a girl without feeling very uncomfortable. If he had to talk to a girl, even about something totally impersonal, he would blush and his hand would shake, and his conversation would either be nonexistent or he would make a fool of himself. He never did himself justice in any of his dealings with girls, and as a result he never had the courage to ask a girl out, or even to have the most benign and innocent of social involvements with a member of the opposite sex. If he went to a party or a disco, he would be so uncomfortable that he felt as though he would literally die of embarrassment.

The result of all this was that he had become something of a recluse. He avoided all situations where he might be forced into the company of girls. That might have been all right if he had disliked girls, but he was like most other boys, he had a healthy interest in members of the opposite sex and would have given just about anything to have had a girlfriend. Of all people, he really needed a girlfriend because having a girlfriend would give him confidence, but his problem stopped him from getting one. He had reached the stage where he felt that no girl could possibly be interested in him because he appeared to be such a fool.

Michael was anything but a fool. In every way, apart from his shyness, he was very competent and able, and he was very attractive. He should have been fighting girls off, but in fact he was probably discouraging them, and all because of his shyness. It was a great waste of his youth. Michael's problems might well have come right in time. No doubt he would meet the 'right' woman eventually, and probably cease to be so shy, but why should he wait for fate to intervene at some unspecified time in the future whilst his life ticked away? Michael wanted help now, and the discussion which he and I then had about his problem was the start of that help. Michael was able to overcome his shyness, but it took time and effort. As far as Michael was concerned, the expenditure of that time and effort was worthwhile.

We will look later at the methods Michael used to overcome his shyness, but for now let's just accept that he had a problem, and that there were techniques which he could use to overcome it. You can overcome just about anything if you go about it the right way.

Shyness can be at its most painful when one is young. It can afflict boys and girls with equal severity, and its effects can be devastating. It can be much more than a minor irritation, it can be a serious disability, but it can be equally serious for an older person. Again it can cause problems at work and in one's social life. Let's consider another person's problem.

Elizabeth

Elizabeth was 23 when I met her first. I was doing a medical examination on her for the engineering firm for which she worked. She had had many absences and her employer had requested the examination in an effort to sort out the problem and perhaps avoid dismissing her. It had been made clear to her that this was her last chance. A lot depended upon what happened at this medical examination, so I was prepared to take a lot of time and give her every chance to explain her problem, not just in her interest, but because she was a good employee and her employer would have been sorry to lose her.

Elizabeth's absences had been due to a variety of minor illnesses, but it was obvious that there was an over-riding problem which she wasn't telling me about. She was restless and anxious, and on occasions evasive. She worked in the wages office and she enjoyed that, but as we talked I began to wonder if she did enjoy her work as much as she claimed to. After a while I was sure that there was something she wasn't telling me about and so I asked her a direct question. Just what was her problem in the wages office? Was it her immediate boss? Was she having problems with the work? After a few more questions Elizabeth broke down and cried, and whilst I hoped I hadn't pushed her too far, we had at least got to the root of her difficulty.

It seemed that the wages office was staffed by a small group of young women who all knew each other and who all got on very well together. There was a lot of laughter and joking, frequent practical jokes and a great spirit of camaraderie. Elizabeth felt like an outsider. She found it difficult to join in, and so the others treated her as an oddity and she became the butt of most of the jokes. Without any prompting from me she told me that she had always been shy, and that she saw her problem in the office as being one of excessive shyness. She wanted to join in, to be friends with the rest of the women, but she simply couldn't. She was too shy.

After we had broached the subject of shyness, Elizabeth relaxed and talked more freely. It was a subject she wanted

to talk about because it was the basis, not only of her problem at work, but also of many other problems she had in
her everyday life and in her social life. We talked about it,
came to some conclusions, and decided that we could do
something about it. We will talk more about what we were
able to do later.

Another individual whom I came to know was older, and
although shyness is often thought of as being something
that mainly afflicts the young, it can affect older people. As
you go through life, we learn how to compensate for many
of the problems which bother us, and in many ways life
becomes easier, but when circumstances change, or we are
in unfamiliar circumstances or we are stressed by bereave-
ment or loss of job, old problems which were inadequately
dealt with can again emerge. A friend of mine found himself in such a situation.

John

John was an old friend in both senses of the word 'old'. He
had been a friend of mine for many years, and he was
elderly. He had been happily married for over forty years,
but three years previously his wife had died after a long illness. At the time John had been devastated by her death,
and some people thought that he would never recover, but
recover he did, and in time he settled down to what should
have been a happy and contented old age.

John did seem to be happy, but people soon noticed that
he didn't go out as much as he once had, and then that he
didn't go out at all. He became almost housebound, relying
on friends and neighbours to do his shopping for him. If he
did go out it was always a brief journey to the nearest
shops. He didn't go to visit his family, no matter how much
they begged him to go, even though he seemed to have no
excuse. Eventually everyone became worried about him
and I was asked to have a word with him and try to sort
things out.

My old friend didn't want to talk about his problems. It
was a long time before he was persuaded to discuss them,
and even then John didn't have words to describe what was

wrong. He certainly didn't use the word 'shy', yet the best way of describing John's situation seemed to be to say that he had become shy in the presence of others, even, or perhaps particularly, members of his own family. He didn't want to visit his son or his daughter because he felt so uncomfortable in their houses. It was a great shame, because now he rarely saw his grandchildren.

We sat and talked long into the evening, and as we talked the true nature of his problem came to light. When he was in the company of others he experienced the sort of physical sensations which shy people will know only too well. He felt embarrassed and uneasy, he was uncomfortable in shops and to his great distress, he felt uncomfortable in the company of his children and grandchildren. As a result of this uneasiness, he avoided the company of others and had become something of a recluse. It wasn't that he didn't want to mix with other people, it's just that he found it difficult.

One could speculate about the nature of John's problems, but they were clearly not unconnected with the death of his wife, and the loneliness and desolation which followed that. Talking about his problems helped, and there were other things which we could do to alleviate the suffering which his shyness was now causing.

The problems these three people experienced were all different. Shyness is usually thought of as something which particularly afflicts young people, but anyone can be shy. It may be worse for young people because of the social lives they lead, (or are expected to lead), where they are always out and about meeting others, and because they are expected to conform, and because they haven't yet developed ploys which help them to disguise their shyness. Shyness may be worse for young people, but it can affect anyone and it can be distressing for anyone.

What next?

If your shyness is not causing you any problems, if you regard it as a pleasant or attractive characteristic, then what follows in this book is of casual interest only. If however, you feel that your shyness makes your life miserable, if it holds you back, if it stops you from doing even one thing that you would like to be doing but feel that you can't, you might consider doing something about it. If shyness is ruining your life, then you owe it to yourself to do something about it, and to do it soon because you are wasting your life.

Of course, shyness is a difficult thing to get to grips with. It has a psychological and a physical component, and it has all sorts of social implications. Shyness can be specific, related to one aspect of your life—often to do with relationships between the sexes—but no matter how shyness affects you, you can improve your situation and you owe it to yourself to work towards that end. It isn't easy, but the first step is to understand your problem. In the next chapter we will start to think about shyness in more detail, and try to understand just what shyness really is.

REMEMBER:

- Shyness can be a serious problem. It can affect every part of your life, and it can change your life by limiting what you can do, both socially and in other situations.
- It tends to be worse for young people, but anyone can be shy, and anyone can become shy if their situation changes.
- You can also become less shy, and there are ways of making yourself feel less shy.
- It is worthwhile taking on your problem because if you overcome your shyness the quality of your life will improve.

Chapter 2

Learning about shyness

How much do you know about shyness? Are you a shy person? If you are, just how shy are you, and how did that shyness develop? Do you want to do something about it, and if you do, do you know how to go about overcoming it? These are important questions, and unless you can answer them, you will continue to lead a life diminished by a condition which *can* be overcome and defeated. All it takes is determination and a little self-knowledge, so you don't have to be shy.

Are you shy?

That might seem to be a very straightforward question. Of course you're shy: that's why you are reading this book. But how do you judge your shyness? The only real way is to compare yourself with others, because shyness is relative. That is to say, everyone is capable of feeling shy, everyone is capable of feeling embarrassed, everyone has their grim memories of times when they wished the floor had opened and swallowed them up, when embarrassment was acute and terrible. Is your shyness better or worse than other people's? Perhaps it is just that your shyness is different from theirs? The answers to these questions may seem to be simple at first glance, but then you probably haven't asked them before, so you may never have really challenged the basic presumptions of your shyness.

Well, isn't everyone shy? All that you know about what other people feel is what they choose to tell you, and people are the most dreadful liars. Of course you can observe people, look at what they do, and perhaps note that they seem to be more outgoing or more competent than you are, more socially aware and more at ease in a whole range of situations. That is the way it seems to be, and it is possible that they *are* more competent, but could it be that they feel just as bad as you, except that they deal with their internal churnings more successfully than you do?

Common sense would suggest that things aren't so simple and that we are all made differently, so that while almost everyone can feel shy on occasion, a truly shy person will feel shy most of the time so that shyness is a real problem for him or her. A brash, outgoing person still has the ability to be shy and uncomfortable sometimes, but he or she is happy and comfortable most of the time and in most social situations. Shyness isn't an absolute thing, so you can't simply say that some people are shy and some aren't. Shyness is a spectrum of feelings, emotions, and physical sensations which everyone can experience. In that way shyness isn't like an illness which you are born with or which you can catch. It is just an exaggeration of something common to all humanity. People understand shyness because they have experienced some part of it.

That, of course, doesn't mean that they will all make allowances for shyness or treat a shy person sympathetically. If it is a characteristic of shy people that they think about others and care possibly too much about what others think of them, it is a characteristic of brash people that they exploit others, often because they are too concerned about their own lives and ambitions to worry about anyone else. At best, people just don't think, so as a shy person you are left to deal with your own problems. That means tackling the many sides of your shyness in as many ways as you can, but first you have to understand what your shyness is and how it affects you. First, know your enemy.

Other problems

You might like to consider some other conditions which are similar to shyness in many ways. One such condition is known as an anxiety state, which could be thought of as an extreme form of shyness. In an anxiety state all those physical symptoms which a shy person might experience in some situations are present, but in an anxiety state they are present all the time, so that someone suffering from this condition will feel anxious all the time. It is the physical side of the condition which predominates: distressing symptoms may be present much of the time, such as a tremor, or muscle tension giving rise to headaches and other muscle pain, or diarrhoea. They are the same sort of symptoms one might suffer if one was confronted by danger, but of course there is no physical danger.

The symptoms are produced by stress, which is a psychological phenomenon, but the result of the stress is a physical condition. You might recognize some of the similarities this condition has to severe shyness. As you know very well, a shy person can also experience physical symptoms before a party or some stressful event, but those symptoms don't predominate and they aren't as severe as they would be for a person suffering from an anxiety state. Yet there is a common thread running through both conditions, that of a psychological state associated with physical symptoms which anyone might experience in certain difficult situations. Understanding this will help you defeat your shyness.

Everyone can feel shy or anxious, but some people feel shy or they may feel anxious all the time. It is a matter of degree, an exaggeration of the normal experience; it is no reflection on our worth as human beings or on our ability to do our jobs or to be attractive or desirable to members of the opposite sex. There is nothing strange or different about a shy person.

Let's consider another human phenomenon so common that everyone has experience of it either in themselves or in someone they know. That phenomenon is a phobia, but what do we mean by a phobia? You may think you know, but here is one definition which you might not have considered. A phobia is the sudden experience of severe sensations by an individual confronted by something which they find threatening. It is an irrational fear, and that fear is expressed by the experience of an increased heart rate, sweating, tummy churning and many other physical symptoms. These symptoms come on suddenly when you see a mouse, perhaps, or are in an aircraft, or in any one of hundreds of different situations. A phobia is really the experience of acute severe anxiety in response to a particular stimulus.

You can see that there is a great similarity between an anxiety state and a phobia. In one, generalized anxiety produces physical symptoms; in the other the physical symptoms are produced in specific situations. Shyness is similar to these conditions, but to a much lesser degree. It is a state of mind, of course, but it is associated with physical sensations and you will certainly have experienced some of these.

What shy person hasn't had sweaty palms or a fast-beating heart, or had difficulty swallowing? In a way it is like a phobia, but the stimulus is not a mouse or a spider, but rather the company of others. Social events, parties, meetings or dates are all the same. They are 'sweaty palm events' where your heart beats as if it were trying to escape from your chest, and an event which should be entirely enjoyable becomes a nightmare. It's something a shy person lives with every day in life. It is associated with a state of mind in which public encounters are perceived as being unpleasant so that the sufferer becomes reticent, perhaps even avoiding public events.

How does it happen?

Which comes first, the physical discomfort or the mental anguish? How does it happen anyway? Perhaps we are just born shy and that is that, there really isn't anything we can do about it. In fact that's only partly true. We are all born different, and some of us are born more shy than others—often because our parents are shy—and we can do nothing about that. But other aspects of shyness are learned, not the way you learn in school, but learned subconsciously in many unhappy experiences and encounters. It is a great whirlpool of learned physical responses, an understandable reticence and a gradual loss of confidence which threatens to suck you down.

Much of your shyness is something which develops over the years, and so it must be something that we can learn. That is the key to overcoming it, because something which has been learned can also be unlearned with equal success. As you go through life you do learn how to survive your shyness and no one is ever completely overwhelmed by it, but you can do better than that. You can learn to overcome your shyness if you understand it, see how it has developed, and if you go about overcoming it the right way. Let's consider how Michael, the young man we met in the last chapter, learned about his shyness.

Michael

Michael's shyness didn't come out of the blue, although it had only really become a problem over the last few years. That was when his interest in girls became important to him and his shyness started to affect his everyday life so that he now really wanted to do something about his problem. That was an important first step in overcoming it, but he wanted to know what to do next and was desperate for help.

I was able to reassure him that there were things that he could do, and that they were straightforward practical measures rather than any esoteric procedures. There's nothing mystical or mysterious about shyness so a simple down-to-earth attitude to it is by far the best approach. I think that was reassuring to Michael. Just the same, it was important for him to fully understand his shyness, in relation to both his past and his future, so a little time spent in the dissection of his shyness would be worthwhile.

For a start, Michael really did think that his shyness had come out of the blue. He had blotted out all those miserable experiences of his childhood and was not eager to go back over them. When he was asked to do so, he experienced again the pain of the many incidents where shyness had intruded into his life, but his memory was good, and he could remember incidents where he had been made a figure of fun, or where he had made a fool of himself because of his clumsiness. I asked him to write down his worst recollection and it turned out to be a very upsetting event for a shy young child to go through. He had gone to a new primary school, and his shyness had prevented him from asking the teacher if he could go to the toilet, with the inevitable result that he wet himself, and everyone knew and laughed at him. It was a time of severe crushing mental agony, something which marked him for life. That was only one of many miserable occasions at school, Sunday school and other places where he was bullied or embarrassed, where shyness played a part and where his shyness was nurtured.

I asked Michael to write down some of his past experiences, not in order to cause him pain and distress, but rather to help him to see how his shyness had developed and how he had learned to compensate for it; in this way he could understand himself and his problem better. It became clear to me and to Michael that he had faced many difficulties in his life, even as a child, with great courage, and that he had overcome many problems on the strength of that courage alone. Michael was no minor player in the game of life; he was someone with a handicap which he dealt with courageously. He had learned to play it down over the years, just so that life could go on. In many ways this had been successful, but one result of this was that he had skirted round his problem and avoided taking it on. As a child that is all he could do because he didn't have the knowledge to do more, but now as an adult he wanted a better quality of life and he was determined to get it.

Writing things down

You may remember that in the first chapter I suggested that you write down the events of a typical day so that you could better see how shyness affected you. Writing things down helps to clarify them in your mind. It forces you to be specific about events, and if you are embarking on a journey of self-discovery you need to be clear in your thinking. You need know who you are and to have a realistic appraisal of yourself as you were, as you are now and then you have to decide what you can become. Writing things down is a tool which you can use to overcome your shyness, and you will use it over and over again as you go on.

Your childhood

Why not have a look at your childhood? It doesn't matter what age you are now—it is in your childhood that so many of your attitudes were formed, your habits of behaviour developed and your body's physical responses learned. Shyness is a combination of these elements, so we learned our shyness in childhood, perhaps starting as a timid infant hiding behind our mother's legs. That's nothing to be ashamed of or to worry about. That is the hand we were dealt, what we are interested in from now on is how we have played it, and how we are going to play it in the future.

Recalling difficult times in one's childhood has its dangers. When you remember unpleasant events you experience again the anguish which you felt then, that feeling of despair which you have banished from your mind. You feel sorry for yourself all over again, but that isn't entirely negative. We want to create a mood of gritty realism, even of anger about the unhappiness your shyness has caused you. Start writing.

Let's begin the exercise by going backwards from the notes we made in the last chapter about a day in our lives when shyness caused us problems, and remember a previous occasion not too long ago when we suffered from our shyness. That won't be too difficult. It might have been a time when you put your foot in it whilst talking to somebody of the opposite sex and made a fool of yourself simply because you felt awkward or embarrassed because you were shy. Or you might have said the wrong thing in company and accidentally insulted someone. The recollection of these incidents makes us squirm with embarrassment even years after the event. It might be interesting to imagine how different such an event might have been if you hadn't been shy. How would you have handled it then? Try to write that down too.

Try to go further back into childhood, and make a note about an event which you remember because you were shy. It might be a children's party where the children were playing a kissing game, or where you were asked to do your party piece. You know that feeling of dread, the certain knowledge that this was a situation you just couldn't handle, and you may remember the physical torture you felt as well. The agony for a shy child is even worse than it is for an adult because a child has no way of dealing with it. A child just suffers, and often suffers in silence, not wanting to tell a parent because even for a child shyness is a secret agony, something not to be discussed.

How did shyness affect you at school? Were you bullied, or made a figure of fun, or were you harassed by sadistic teachers? It wouldn't do to exaggerate, but these things do happen to shy children, and when they do they become etched on to both our conscious and subconscious selves, so that we remember them and our bodies also learn to respond adversely to similar situations in the future; because of this it is difficult for the shy child to avoid becoming the shy adult. Write it down. Why not? We want to remember, underline and understand the events of the past which have contributed to our current state.

What is the first 'shy event' you can remember? Some people can think right back to very early childhood and remember something related to their shyness, and the memory will still be painful. It is easy to see how such early painful experiences make us wary of similar experiences in the future. Something which has been unpleasant once will surely be unpleasant again, and you will be able to trace a thread of shyness through most of the experiences of your childhood right up to adolescence, when the dawn of sexual awareness turns the pain of shyness into agony. Writing it down, remembering it, reliving it increases your understanding of the shyness you are experiencing now, so that you achieve a sense of the continuity of your shyness from your earliest experiences to the present day.

Take the time to chart the progress of your shyness from its beginning up to the present day, because by doing so you will have to confront the reality of your shyness now, something you may have been avoiding. You may have been able to do that by learning to compensate for your shyness either by avoiding situations which make you feel shy, either physically or by closing your mind to them, or by making excuses to yourself, but in so doing you are living less of your life than you could be.

Your upbringing

There must have been other influences which affected the development of your shyness during your childhood years, and one of those influences was that of your upbringing. Parents do their best to bring children up to be ideal citizens, well-equipped to deal with life's difficulties, but there is no rule book and every parent, and therefore every child, learns the hard way. Most parents simply react to the problems their children bring to them, and respond according to their experience of life. If a mother or father has no experience of shyness, they may find that difficult. Even if the parents are shy themselves, they may respond by trying to overcompensate for their child's shyness, or even by trying to force the child to be less shy in an attempt to spare the child the torment of shyness which they experienced, and may still experience.

There are other possible problems with families. Each family is a unit with an identity and character of its own. Some families close ranks against the outside world, and whilst 'close' families may be admirable in many ways, they can be very introspective and deny a child its independence of thought, so that normal development is impeded. There are other family problems, that of the overbearing father, or the ineffectual father or mother, or the dominating mother beloved of Jewish comedians, all of which may intimidate or exploit the already shy child and make his or her problems worse.

Few parents deliberately exploit the shyness of a child, but some parents aren't very good at being parents and just don't go about things the right way, with the result that the shy child simply becomes more shy, learning the wrong lessons in the home. The firm encouragement and reassurance needed for normal development is absent, perhaps because parents have too much trouble dealing with their own lives, or too little knowledge or insight to respond appropriately to the problems of their children. There's no point in blaming parents, or even feeling resentful if these things happened in your family; if, for example, your parents didn't get on with each other and your house was miserable as a result, it is your parents who were the main victims, not you. And who's to say that you wouldn't have been just as shy if you had come from an ideal home, and who is to say what an ideal home is anyway? It is better to accept the status quo and get on with life, but looking at your family life may help you to understand how you came to be where you are today, and it may give you some insight into your current problems.

It might be of interest to look again at the case of Elizabeth.

Elizabeth

We met Elizabeth in the last chapter. She was bullied at her work in a wages office, but in many other ways she was very outgoing and would not have thought of herself as being particularly shy. During our conversation we talked about her childhood, and some interesting facts came to light. She was the second oldest child in a family of five. Her father had died in an accident when she was twelve and the family had to get on with their lives as best they could; a strong family relationship had developed between the three boys and two girls.

Elizabeth had held her own, and had been close to her mother and her brothers and sisters, and it seemed to be a normal close-knit family. When she was asked to remember incidents and events which might relate to her shyness, she mentioned one occasion which she remembered very well. (It is surprising how clearly we can recall events of our childhood if we really try. Events and images come back as if they have happened yesterday.) Elizabeth remembered being at the seaside with her brothers and sisters when an argument developed about a game on the beach. She had taken a strong stand, but the others had united against her and she had been ostracized, not just for that day, but for the rest of the holiday so that she spent days alone and unhappy until her mother intervened.

This wasn't an isolated event; there were other occasions when the family closed ranks against her in the way that children do. There was no lasting malice, but Elizabeth did always tend to be the odd one out. This was something which she hadn't really realized until she was forced to think about it. It is possible that when Elizabeth is stressed, her shyness reappears and becomes a problem in the way it has been in the past.

It would be a mistake to read too much into Elizabeth's past problems. She had probably always been a shy child, and her experiences within her family may have accentuated this shyness. By looking at her previous experiences she was able to get some insight into her current problems, which hadn't exactly come out of the blue as she had thought—her experiences in her office were just a continuation of something which had happened before. It was something she had learned to live with, and she would learn to live with again, but this time using more informed and relevant techniques which would help her to confront her problem and overcome it, so that it wouldn't keep re-emerging in difficult times.

Not all experiences are bad

There are compensations for being shy. Being brash and unselfconscious has its drawbacks even in childhood, so being shy isn't a totally negative experience. Shy children are often sensitive, often aware of the needs of others, often able to enjoy books, music or theatre which other children cannot understand. Shy children do make friends, and there may have been occasions when the drawbacks of shyness were outweighed by its advantages.

It would be wrong to start with a totally negative scenario. If we are to write down recollections of our past let's try to compensate for the bad with some recollections of the good. It might be a time on holiday when you met another child and made a friendship which was close and valuable, where you understood each other's values and each recognized the quality of the other. The compensations of shyness often come in the form of human relationships because the shy person can understand the needs and frailties of others.

Even if your shyness led to loneliness, itself a terrible affliction, there are compensations in the form of self-fulfilment and the pleasure of reading and enjoying subtleties denied to others. You might not choose to be shy, you might not wish shyness on your worst enemy, but you can admit even grudgingly that shyness has some compensations which extend into adult life. Let's not deny them or underestimate them. Mark them down on the plus side.

Managing your shyness

Let's not spend too much time immersed in the past. It's interesting to do that, but also a little self-indulgent. What we really should be interested in is the future, and although things which have happened in the past certainly affect our prospects and cannot be ignored, shyness can be overcome no matter how serious a problem it is now, and no matter what difficulties and embarrassments it has caused you in the past.

Shyness cannot be defeated in one night. You cannot just decide that you aren't going to be shy, and there are no short cuts. If you are to achieve a lasting solution you have to do some work yourself, possibly embrace some concepts which you might find difficult, and even expose yourself to some situations which might make you uncomfortable. There simply is no easy way, but the benefits you will achieve from overcoming your shyness far outweigh any effort you may have to put in.

The reassuring fact is that there's nothing wrong with your mind or anything else about you. You are shy—that is all. You were born that way and you can see how the situation has developed over the years as shyness breeds shyness in a nasty self-replicating circle, but you don't have to put up with that. There are practical ways of overcoming the problem. You can't change the way you think or the way you feel, but you can change the way you act and the way you dress, for example, so the way forward has to be practical, down-to-earth and sensible. Face up to your shyness as a simple fact of life without any emotional overtones. Get your remorse over missed opportunities in the past out of the way now, treat your shyness simply as a problem to be tackled and overcome, and you are on the right path.

REMEMBER:

- You were born shy, like many other people.
- Experiences in your life have made your shyness worse, and you have spent many miserable hours as a result.
- You can't ignore them or forget about them, but don't let them interfere with your future.
- There are many practical things you can do to first manage your shyness and then overcome it.

Chapter 3

Shyness and personality

As far as most people are concerned, if someone is shy, their whole personality is governed by their shyness: it's the shyness which is important, which predominates, so that the other aspects of that person's personality seem to take second place.

Shyness is really a private agony, but its outward manifestations are sometimes so obvious that people notice. We feel our shyness; other people see our shyness. That isn't necessarily bad because shyness can be attractive to other people, but in some situations it can also be a disadvantage. Shy people aren't the most competitive in the world, or they may not appear to be competitive and others may seek to take advantage of what they see as a weakness.

It's all very well to say that shyness is attractive, but most shy people would give almost anything not to be shy. They don't feel attractive, and they don't want to be passive participants when it comes to forming relationships, or simply to be unable to form relationships at all. They would like to be competitive and confident, and no one wants to be pitied or condescended to. A shy person wants to meet others on equal terms. Shy people are embarrassed by their shyness.

Facing the fact that shyness often has external manifestations gives us one way of tackling the problem. We want to make practical changes which will help us to overcome our shyness, and we can change some of these external clues to our shyness. More about that later, but now we must look at other practical aspects of our shyness so that we can see how we can alter these to our advantage. We really must understand ourselves, so let's look at the relationship between our shyness and the rest of our personality.

Our shyness and our true selves

We have considered other conditions which resemble shyness, things like anxiety states or even phobias. They resemble shyness in that they have a physical side as well as a psychological side, but in other ways they are different. One could say that so-and-so 'suffers from an anxiety state'. One could say that somebody suffers from depression, another psychological condition with physical manifestations, but when it comes to shyness you say that someone *is* shy. Shyness is their 'label'. Shyness is seen as the way they are: not something which is tacked on to their personality, but something which runs through every aspect of their being. I wonder if that is true or if it is fair?

If you are shy you will have your own opinions about these things, but if you are shy you may well regard your shyness with unnecessary pessimism. Psychologists spend a lot of time categorizing and typing personality, but we won't do that here because we don't want to get bogged down in too much detail. Common sense suggests that shy people, like everyone else, come in all shapes and sizes, in all types of personality and with all sorts of different talents and abilities. A shy person can be just as effective and as competitive as anyone else. The problem is that other people may not recognize that, and even worse, shy people themselves can find it hard to believe. Shyness can dominate your personality and hide your real self.

Shyness certainly permeates many different parts of the personality. It is a thread which runs through your confidence, your feeling of worth, your sense of fulfilment, all sorts of things. Shyness is all-pervading, and if you interviewed ten shy people there would be some things they would have in common. They would certainly be recognizable as being shy, but behind that facade of shyness there would be ten very different people trying to get out. If shyness is a prison the bars will look the same from the outside, but inside each individual is his or her own personality.

That isn't quite the whole story. Shyness is more than just a facade, more than a public face we show the world. Shyness does affect every aspect of our personality, but it isn't an integral part of that personality. It is just that our personality is touched by the presence of our shyness, almost as if the shyness was imposed from outside. All aspects of our personality are repressed, and as a result that shyness is reflected in the way we act so that others can say that we are shy. Shyness is a secret which is hard to keep.

Shyness is not then a fundamental part of our personality. It is simply one aspect, but it does have far-reaching implications concerning the way we feel and the way we behave. It can assume huge proportions and can come to dominate our lives so that we begin to think of ourselves as being shy and nothing else. We lose sight of our true selves, and if we are to overcome our shyness we have to redis-cover our true selves, put our shyness into its proper perspective, and then set about diminishing its importance until it becomes a trivial annoyance. We can do that by working at the edges of our shyness, whittling it away without affect-ing any aspect of our true personality. Or we might think of shyness as a thread which runs through so many aspects of our personality, a thread which can be teased out and removed. It is in no way an integral part of our true selves, no matter how entrenched it may appear to be.

Because shyness is so all-pervading it affects many parts of our personality and thus every aspect of our lives. What was a difficulty in childhood, an annoyance, becomes an intolerable strain in adolescence, and then settles down to the dead weight of a never-ending impediment for the rest of our lives—unless we do something about it. It might be worthwhile taking a close look at some other people's problems now because the time is approaching when you will start to deal with your shyness, start to separate your shyness from the rest of your personality with the precision of a surgeon's knife, and if you are to do that you must know precisely what you are dealing with.

Graham

Graham was sixteen. He didn't come to see me of his own accord: he was brought by his worried mother. That isn't a very good start to any consultation because if the individual is reluctant to seek help there is little possibility of giving help. On this occasion that wasn't quite the case. Graham initially denied that he needed help, but when his mother had left he was prepared to discuss his problems and ended up staying for a long time. He had a lot to discuss.

His mother had told me that he was shy. He had always been shy, but now it was a real problem. His shyness had led him to become withdrawn so that he was now a total recluse. He went to school all right, but he had no outside interests apart from watching television. Television was now his life, and his mother felt that something would have to be done. That may have been true, but the only person who could do something about it was Graham himself. Did he want to change his life?

Graham was reticent at first, but it soon transpired that he was extremely unhappy with his life as he was currently living it, and that all he really wanted to do was to live a normal, fulfilled life like most of his friends. He didn't enjoy being a recluse at all, but keeping himself to himself was the line of least resistance, and it was all that he felt that he could achieve at that time. He had no thoughts about the future at all, apart from a feeling of hopelessness. What had gone wrong?

There could be no quick and easy answers, which is something we all have to learn. There just isn't a 'quick fix'. The first thing we had to do was to find out just what was happening, but in Graham's case that wasn't difficult because there wasn't very much happening in his life. We did discover one important thing though, and that was the fact that Graham wished very much that he could do more and enjoy himself more. He did have a real desire to overcome his shyness. There was one other hopeful fact, and that was that Graham understood that his problems came from his shyness, knew that he was shy and admitted to himself that he was shy. We were off to a flying start.

One thing which Graham and I didn't do was to try to discover deep psychological reasons for his shyness, and although we did consider events in his childhood, that was more for background information than for anything else. The main thing that we achieved at this first meeting was a commitment to work to overcome Graham's shyness, and that commitment had to come principally from him, because he alone held the key which would unlock his real personality and free him from the burden of his shyness.

Graham and I met on many occasions. Graham wasn't doing very much on a day-to-day basis, so it was easy to find things he was avoiding. What I wanted to know was what situations he disliked most, or feared most. What situations did he find just a bit difficult? Not surprisingly, considering Graham's age, the thing which he found made him feel most shy was the thought of any contact with girls. Girls scared the pants off him, and so he had become a non-combatant, a recluse. There was more to his shyness than that, but clearly that was his main difficulty, and the one he wished to address most. Were there things that I wanted Graham to talk about?

I wanted Graham to tell me things about himself, things he didn't normally talk about and things he probably hadn't thought about before. I wanted to know about his opinion of himself, or rather his opinion about the different aspects of himself, because we all have complex personalities. I wondered what he believed other people thought about him. Not surprisingly, many of Graham's opinions were negative. We all know that an optimist is someone who sees a glass as being half full, whereas a pessimist thinks it is half empty. Graham was very much a half empty person. Yet Graham was intelligent and able, talented in many aspects of his life and particularly in his academic work. Graham couldn't see this and was aware only of his poor performance in public due to his lack of social skills. His self-image was poor, and the image he presented to the world was very negative. There were many areas where progress could be made, areas which seemed to be screamingly obvious, but Graham couldn't see them. My task was first to let Graham see his real self, and then to release that self.

The components of shyness

What was getting in the way of Graham's true self? Why had his shyness intervened between himself and the world in which he so much wished to participate? It was a combination of factors, and what was true for Graham is true for every shy person. These factors are closely interrelated and interdependent, each contributing to the actions of the other. We have touched on them already.

When Graham was in a group of people his performance was poor. He didn't speak comfortably, didn't know what to speak about and when he did speak he tended to be too outspoken and gauche. Often he would say the wrong things. When he was asked to do something he was clumsy and awkward, and he had a slight hand tremor. He blushed easily and sweated easily. He never quite knew how much to say, when to speak and when to be quiet, and how much eye contact he should make.

Graham was acutely aware of how poor his performance was, and indeed thought it was much worse than it actually was. An observer might have noticed that Graham was a bit shy, but Graham thought that his public performance was nothing short of a disaster. Over the years he developed a very poor image of himself, and could actually visualize himself as a poor bumbling oaf, a gross exaggeration of what he actually was. His image was of an individual who had no hope. All of his ideas about himself were negative. He looked bad, his performance in public was bad, everything about him was negative, so he had a completely negative—and completely undeserved—self-image. No one could be in the least interested in him, and of course that included girls.

Because Graham had such a poor image of himself and because he thought so little of his public performance, he had a very poor expectation of what his performance would be like in any given situation, and as a result he had a very poor expectation of what he might be able to achieve. He would never ask a girl out because he would anticipate rejection. If he was to go to a dance he would anticipate that for him it would be a disaster. He wouldn't volunteer for a part in a school play, or to make a speech, or for any activity which would make him conspicuous. He expected to feel awkward and to appear awkward.

The result of these attitudes was that his behaviour became a little odd. He did actually sometimes appear a little shifty, and he began to avoid *some* situations, and later *any* situation in which he thought he might feel shy, and in time that became almost all situations. In that way the image he gave to the world was of a very shy, reclusive individual. He dressed modestly, behaved in a self-effacing way and avoided many situations. He tried not to draw attention to himself. The messages he sent out about himself were all about his shyness. Inadvertently he advertised the fact that he was very shy, very prickly and very unapproachable, the opposite of what he wanted to be, and the opposite of what he could be.

As a result of all of these things Graham developed very negative feelings, not only about himself, but about almost everything. He had a poor expectation about how he would perform not only now but also in the future. His view of the world was pessimistic and negative. He would assume that things would turn out badly and had no hope that things might improve. He could not see his future clearly, and did not think that he would do very well.

These negative attitudes and poor expectations led to an even worse performance in public, and something else also contributed to this poor performance. He began to develop very real physical symptoms in public. He had his tremor, his blushing and his sweating, but he could also get diarrhoea and feelings of panic, problems swallowing or breathing, and these physical feelings made him feel conspicuous and so decreased his performance and his expectation of what his performance could be. In short, Graham's shyness had gone from being a childhood difficulty to being a major problem in his life, and a problem which was getting worse.

The impact of Graham's shyness on his life was profound. It took over his life, so that his shyness was everything. His true worth was obscured, his life distorted by this almost overwhelming shyness. Graham was of course an extreme case. Just the same, his problems could be applied in a lesser degree to any person who is shy.

Marianne

Marianne was an acquaintance of mine. She wouldn't have described herself as being shy, and indeed she wasn't overtly bothered by shyness, but I had noticed over many meetings that she didn't manage some things very well. She wasn't good at the 'social graces', seeming awkward and rather loud in public. She was just a little too animated and a little too awkward to appear to be completely at ease. After a party she had given she sat down exhausted and to my surprise asked me why she found these things so difficult.

I shrugged my shoulders. Perhaps she was shy? That was something she hadn't considered. She was too used to being the life and soul of the party to have ever noticed that it took her a tremendous effort to achieve that result. It certainly didn't come naturally to her, and most of her encounters with other people were just as difficult. After she had thought about it she realized that these things were difficult for her, and the reason for her difficulty was just that she was a rather shy person. The company of other people made her uneasy and she had to work very hard to overcome her problem.

Marianne didn't avoid difficult situations. She lived a full and varied life, but she was uncomfortable much of the time and her way of dealing with that was to overcompensate. She just overdid things, talked too loudly, gestured too extravagantly and generally overwhelmed other people. She would never have sought help for her shyness because she didn't really think of it as being a problem, yet there was a difficulty for her, and the fact that she had raised the matter with me suggested that she wasn't altogether unaware of her shortcomings in public. She did want to improve her performance by being more natural and at ease, and that was something we went on to discuss.

Different kinds of shyness

It's true that there are different degrees of shyness rather than different kinds. Shyness is an entity in itself, but it is possible to be more shy in some situations than in others so that there can appear to be different kinds of shyness. Basically, shyness is a combination of the psychological awareness of being ill at ease, the physical sensations of the same thing, and a resulting awkwardness in certain situations. Any one of these factors can predominate, and they can be worse in some situations than in others.

It is possible to be perfectly at ease in a situation you are used to, perhaps in an area where you are competent such as at work, and very uneasy in some other situations, maybe with people of the opposite sex. Shyness can be complex.

Sorting it out

All this can seem very confusing, but you don't need to be confused. Don't dwell on the nature of shyness and all its complexities. What you really need to do is to get on with the business of sorting it out, finding out what is going on in your life and then producing a plan of campaign so that you can really do something about it. You can see that there are physical and psychological aspects of your shyness and that it is a little complicated, and that may seem daunting. Don't worry. We have a long way to go yet but we will get there, and we will do it in small steps. Each step is simple, but the steps add up to a programme which will allow you first come to terms with your shyness and then get rid of it altogether.

The first part of any programme for overcoming a problem is to understand that problem, and that means understanding your own particular problem which may be different in its detail from anyone else's. You have to find a way of looking at it, breaking it down into its different parts which will make it manageable, and then working on the problem in small pieces. Any problem can be tackled in this way, but you have to have a system, and you have to follow the system. The first question is, where do you start? You have to find some place where the problem is accessible, find something that you can do, and one thing that might be worth trying is keeping a diary.

Keeping a diary

You can only sort out something you understand. You have gone some of the way down the road to understanding already by looking at the way your shyness has developed, but now it might be a good idea to look closely at how shyness affects you. The only way to do that is to write it down, and that means keeping a diary. You don't need to go out and buy a diary, an ordinary piece of writing paper or your notebook will do, but you must be conscientious and record everything which happens in a week, and do it at the time it happens or soon after when it is still fresh in your memory. You have to record everything because you don't yet know in detail how your shyness affects you. Write it down: how you feel, what you think, and how you perform. Underline those events which were affected by shyness, and then look at them in detail.

If some event in a given week did not go as well as you would have liked, why was that? Take a new page and write down the name of that event and underneath write what went right about it, and also what went wrong, and you might be able to add why it went wrong in purely practical terms. How could you have made it go better? What practical steps could you have taken to improve your performance? There's one other thing you should do, and that is to mention any events you may have avoided or not entered into fully because of your shyness. That is of considerable relevance. When you write things down, record the details because it is by attention to detail that you will overcome your shyness.

A young man's diary might look like this:

Monday:

Work by bus. Monday *planning meeting*. Sat at back. Linda did most of the talking for the department. Fairly aggressive discussion with Jack being high-handed as usual.

Lunch in cafeteria with Linda and Brian. Quite comfortable but Linda intimidating. Would have liked to say more. Quiet afternoon.

Pub with Brian and Andy. No problems. Dinner in flat and evening in front of TV.

Tuesday:

Uncomfortable because have interview with client. Edgy on bus. Simply can't stand *McPhee*...he makes me look like an idiot. Interview as usual...unreasonable demands with no explanations accepted. Still, the customer is always right. Evening—party at Andy's girlfriend's. No one to take so go alone. Good crowd but few girls on their own. Chatted up a nice girl called Joanne but got nowhere. *Felt an idiot.* I'm just no good at it. Had a few beers. Home early.

...et cetera.

Now the keeper of this diary might want to look at those areas where his shyness caused problems, and he might want to consider ways in which he might have managed those situations better. He has already underlined the parts he wants to look at in more detail, so that he could make some more notes:.

Planning meeting. Kept a low profile probably because anticipated Jack would be sarcastic. Let Linda take the flak.... but then she got the credit. She can handle it and I can't. It's my department so I should have been able to sit up front and run the show. I should resolve to do that and then find out ways of doing it.

Linda at lunch. Awkward not because Linda is a girl but because she can manage things and I can't. She just dominates the conversation. I should be more assertive.

Interview with client. McPhee just steamrollers me. I have no defence. I just have to learn to be as rude as he is. If I was, would he back off?

Party. Same old trouble. I sound like someone else, some bumbling idiot. Perhaps some girl will see past my awkwardness and see what I'm really like. Maybe I can do better, present myself better. That means being less shy. How do you achieve that? I must do something.

What can you do?

Your brief diary may be nothing like the one above, but it should contain the same elements and similar problems, and it might even contain similar comments on shortcomings and failings. What can you do? How can you become less shy? It can't be done by just wishing. It can't be done by a psychological trick, and it can't be done by anyone but you, but it can be done.

Firstly, it can be done by effort, effort put into dissecting and understanding the way your shyness works in relation to the situations you encounter and the people you meet. It can be done by changing those practical things which can be changed, and after all that, and after progress has been made, by replacing your negative attitudes with more positive ones so that you begin to feel less shy as well as behaving in a less shy way. Success breeds success and it also creates confidence.

Why you have to do something

You have put up with your shyness now for many years, perhaps even for your entire life. You know that you can manage it, even if you don't enjoy it. Surely you can continue to manage it, to get by, so why should you want to take the trouble to really take on your problem and make all the effort which will be required? That is something you will have to ask yourself and get very clear in your own mind, because what you will have to do to overcome your shyness won't be easy and it will take time and effort. It is a big commitment, and you really have to want to do it. I can think of several reasons why it is important that you take this problem on.

The first reason is that if you have always been shy you don't know what sort of person you might have been if you hadn't been shy, and you will never know what you might have achieved both in terms of your career or in terms of your relationships. You will live with that uncertainty, and with a feeling that you may have missed something in life, that some part of life may have passed you by.

You will just never know. This may be your only chance of finding out.

Another reason is that shyness is extremely important, too important to simply ignore. We are social animals, and life is made up of all sorts of relationships. We make corporate decisions, we think and feel in groups, as shown by phrases like 'the mood of the nation has changed,' or 'fear swept through the valley.' It isn't just interactions between the sexes which are affected by shyness, it is all sorts of complex group reactions in business, or in clubs, or in families, villages or towns, all these groups of individuals have an identity and the groups have feeling and make decisions. If you are shy you may tend to be on the periphery of such a group, or you may not be a member at all. If that is true you will not be able to make your full contribution and you may lose out personally, or your group will be less effective as a result.

Then of course there are your personal relationships, particularly with members of the opposite sex, and we will say much more about this later. There are the problems of finding a partner, or of having a fulfilled marriage, or at a more basic level, of simply having fun. If your life is less than full, or if you are missing out on any part of life, then you really should take your shyness on and do something about it.

What can we achieve?

I think that we can achieve a great deal. I believe that we can overcome shyness, but we can do more. Shy people are sensitive and often talented people, so your efforts to overcome your shyness shouldn't just be directed to being as efficient or as comfortable in social situations as someone who isn't shy: your goal should be to do *better* than the average person, to develop ways of solving problems which will give you an advantage over other people. You should be able to develop a system which will allow you to use your shyness to your advantage, so that at the end of the day you can be a winner, a more confident and able person than the other people who now seem to have the advantage over you.

Can you do it? That depends on you, but it is worth try-ing—it is worth the effort.

REMEMBER:

- Shyness is only part of your personality.
- It can affect most aspects of your personality, but it can be separated out and dealt with, releasing your true self.
- Shyness also produces poor self-esteem, a poor image in public, and a poor public performance.
- It can be overcome by practical methods. You can achieve a great deal if you are determined.

Chapter 4

Image

If you spend too long thinking about all the different aspects of shyness it can be very disheartening. Where do you start? How can you make any impact on it? It all seems to be just too difficult, yet you have to begin somewhere. If you are going to overcome your shyness you have to do something. So where can you start? Let's take an arbitrary point in the complex mish-mash which is our shyness. Let's not attempt the impossible by trying to change the way we think or the way we feel. Let's do the practical thing and change something that can be changed.

If shyness permeates most parts of our personality it is obviously going to be difficult to take it on, so let's tackle it at a point where it is accessible. If we start at the peripheries of our shyness we can pare it away from the more fundamental parts of our personality, and if we can be successful in our first efforts we can gain in confidence and proceed more comfortably to the next stage.

We have agreed that the shy person sends out signals which say that he or she is shy. Gestures, the way we dress, our body language, the things we say, all tell people about ourselves and they may say that we are shy. If other people know that we are shy, they react in a way which indicates that they realize we are shy, and that makes our shyness worse. If we radiated confident messages, our exchanges with others would be different. Would that be an improvement in our situation, or a start at least to overcoming our shyness? Anyway, it would be nice to appear less gauche and clumsy in difficult situations. Have you ever thought about changing your image?

Making changes

The idea of making changes to your image might rightly fill you with horror. You might think of a character in a TV sitcom dressing up in hiking gear to try to impress a member of the opposite sex, when the audience knows he actually hates the outdoors. It is a standard TV joke to have someone arrive dressed in a completely different and ludicrous way, pretending to be someone they aren't. It just isn't practical or proper to change yourself by changing the way you dress, but that isn't what I'm suggesting. I'm talking about something much more subtle, much more reasonable and practical, and something which is certainly attainable.

The point is that you have to do something, and if you are to keep working at your shyness you have to do something which gets results and which doesn't take the rest of your life. You can do that by starting to change your image. Why should you be so sceptical about changing your image? It's something which politicians and others do, and there is a whole industry of public relations people and image makers. People in the public eye will often go to great lengths to change their image, using speech and clothing consultants to change totally the way they look, talk and act in public. Whatever we may think of it, it's something which happens.

In a way shy people are in the public eye all the time, or at least that's the way they feel. They feel conspicuous, feel that people are looking at them and sometimes act as if that were the case. Changing the way you behave is very difficult, but there are ways that you can change the image you present of yourself so that you will appear less shy, and the magic is that if you know that you appear less shy you will feel less shy, so the transformation will have begun.

What is image?

Image is just that thing which we present to the world, something that we ourselves create out of ourselves, and in an ideal world it would exactly represent the person we are. Somehow changing that image gives the impression that we are creating something false, but that isn't necessarily the case. After all, what is our true self? Even if we can accurately define the person we really are, does the image we project really represent that person? Do we really know what our image is? We don't see it, and other people don't tell us what it's like. Changing our image might just mean altering our image so that it comes to more accurately represent ourselves.

So our image, that combination of dress, mannerisms, gestures and speech, is something we have to think about, and it is something which we can change voluntarily. We have to proceed with the utmost caution because the potential for disaster is always there. We can always make things worse, always make a fool of ourselves, but we can just as easily make a start to overcoming our shyness by telling other people something about ourselves which may be more satisfactory than what we are telling them at the moment.

What is your image now?

You may have never really considered the way you appear to others, or you may have worked very hard to achieve a particular effect, but you don't know what that effect looks like to other people. The chances are that you are just like everyone else, and dress and behave naturally, or in a way that comes naturally to you without necessarily striving to achieve anything. If you signal something to other people, you may not be aware of just what that signal is and how it is received.

What you do in the way of image-making may be quite unconscious. You may not naturally want to attract attention to yourself, so you may dress quietly and demurely, presenting a grey face to the world. We aren't talking now about taste in clothes, or dress sense, except to the extent that these things are informed by our personality. In your case there may be an overlay of shyness which intervenes between yourself and the image you might like to present to the world, so that your appearance may be less extrovert or less flamboyant than you really are yourself.

You may or may not agree with this concept, but it is certainly something which is worth thinking about, and you might start with one small test. You need an important device to assist you—a mirror. Have a look at yourself in a full-length mirror and take stock of yourself. Look not just at your clothes, look at your posture, look at the whole effect. What you see may be completely satisfactory. We don't deliberately dress to displease ourselves, and the effect you see is probably what you wish to see, but is it creating the effect you really wish it to create? More importantly, could you dress differently just to achieve a slightly different effect?

Of course not everyone who is shy dresses as a mouse, and some of us may dress extravagantly so that our appearance gives no hint of our underlying shyness, and it is also possible to over-dress, to over-compensate for our shyness. You may know of someone who dresses very well and very precisely, giving a sophisticated image when they are really very shy. Their clothes are still not true to their real personality and they may not be able to dress casually when they might be more comfortable in less elaborate clothing, and when it might be more appropriate.

It might be worth trying to change our appearance and our public demeanour just a little, just to bring our image more into line with our true selves.

Finding ourselves

If we are determined to project a more accurate image of ourselves it might be sensible to find out a little more about the personality we are trying to express. Shy people tend to have a slightly distorted impression of themselves: they underestimate themselves and may feel that they are less impressive than they really are. They may also lack confidence, and that can affect the way they dress and the image they present. It takes confidence to make a statement about yourself in the image you present. So what are you really like?

You aren't being asked to indulge in an exercise of self-analysis, but just consider what you are like as a day-to-day person: what things do you like to do, where do you like to go and what sort of entertainment do you enjoy? Are you a casual person or a formal person, and does your dress and your demeanour reflect that, or do you dress defensively? Most people, particularly young people, dress either to conform or else to impress the opposite sex, but their clothes may also say 'Don't touch!' That can be as true for the person who spends hours working to achieve an effect as it is for someone who dresses like a sack of potatoes. If that's the effect you really want to achieve that's fine, but now is the time for complete honesty.

You are by yourself, making your own decisions. You are the only one who can make decisions about yourself, although you can take advice from people you trust. I think it helps to write things down. Try to write down something about the person you are, and then try to write down something about the impression you make in the creation of your image. Are they the same? You may be happy with your image, but could you do just a bit better? Doing a bit better is what we are talking about. A shy girl might write something like this about herself:

'I look at myself in the mirror and I see someone dressed in jeans and a sweater. My hair is short. I have no jewellery, and no make-up because I never have time to do any. I usually dress like this because I look okay, just like everyone else at the college. I don't want to be conspicuous. My appearance is perfectly satisfactory and no one comments on it adversely. I think I look ordinary and that's fine. I could stand straighter, and I suppose I could smile a bit more. Yes, I would like to be noticed a bit more. Other girls do get asked out more than I do, and I have no one to go to the end of term dance with. In class I don't make a great impact, but I don't think that that's because of the way I dress. I would like to be noticed, to make an impact when I sit down at a table for coffee, but I couldn't handle appearing flamboyant, though in a way I would like other people to think that I could be if I wanted. I don't want to appear shy all the time.'

Making changes

We are on the move. We have our shoulder against the dead weight of our shyness and we are going to shift it just a bit. We are going to adjust our image as a first step, but it has to be a small step because the last thing you want is for people to start remarking on the changes you might make. You want to be noticed for yourself, not for your clothes. How would an image maker advise you about your appearance? What factors are involved in making up your appearance?

These factors depend on your sex. Appearance means clothes and shoes, make-up and hair. Image might start from underwear and work out from that. It also includes our posture, the way we walk and talk and the unconscious signals we send out through our mannerisms. An image maker could take anybody to one side and create a *completely* new persona, and for you that would almost certainly be a disaster. We are talking about making small changes, even imperceptibly small changes; these may lead in time to the creation of a different public persona which could be more to our liking because it is more true than the defensive image we now present.

We have already spent time writing down something about the image we present now. The next thing is to write down something about the image we would like to present. Just what sort of effect would you like to have when you walk into a room? This isn't something which can be achieved instantaneously, and it isn't something you would want to achieve instantaneously, but it is something you could work towards in slow stages. It's hard to imagine what you could be like, but it helps if you have someone in mind, either in life or in fiction, whom you might want to be like, someone upon whom you could model yourself.

You cannot, of course, copy someone else. That would produce something entirely phoney. You want to be simply
yourself. The girl in the above example might write something like this:

'There's nothing wrong with jeans and a sweater, but I
certainly don't sparkle. I could have a change of clothes
which wasn't just another pair of jeans. When did I last
wear a skirt? And shoes with a raised heel? I'm not the
tallest person in the world after all. It would help if I
stood up straighter and walked taller. I don't like make-
up, but maybe once in a while I could do something
simple like mascara just to show that I can. I don't want
to wear dangly earrings, but I could wear studs. It would
be nice if someone noticed me occasionally, perhaps
when I wanted them to. It would be nice to have some
style. I wonder what it would feel like to be glamorous?'

How do you go about it?

If you don't feel glamorous it would be a mistake to try to
look glamorous—not right away, that is. If you're going to
make changes in your appearance make them one at a time
and don't try to do too much. Next time you're buying
clothes, take on board the idea that you might buy the
more glamorous option instead of always playing safe. Try
to match your clothes to the occasion and don't be afraid to
dress up once in a while. Be prepared to dress for your
mood, and remember that the subject of clothes includes
underclothes, where you can be glamorous and feel glamorous without anyone knowing.

It is the same for boys—well, almost: boys don't have the
same options in underclothes as girls. And it is the same for
older people. We all have options about our dress, mannerisms and demeanour. We can choose the image we present
to the world, but first we have to know what our image is
now, and then what we would like to change it to, and
lastly, how to go about doing that. It means experimenta-
tion, not just about how we look, but about how we feel
when we change, and what we feel about how we look.

The bottom line of all this is that when you are more comfortable with yourself and you look more relaxed, more confident or whatever, you might just feel a little more relaxed or more confident.

As others see us

A lot of the psychological side of shyness is to do with confidence. If we don't feel confident in company we will feel shy. If we look shy and know that we look shy, it's very difficult to act and behave as if we aren't shy. If on the other hand we know that we look relaxed and confident, it is so much easier to behave as if we are confident. If you dress in a confident way and go to a meeting or to a party and say nothing at all, you will be taken as being confident because that is the image you are projecting. Other people take us at face value. Being shy is hard work, because it's hard to manage in company without appearing awkward and uncomfortable, and that's something we try very hard to avoid. If we can do some of that work with our dress, appearance and demeanour, dealing with our shyness will be so much easier.

So how do others see you now? That isn't easy to say because all opinions are different, but as changing your appearance is a tricky business, at the end of the day it is your own opinion which is important. It's what *you* think of the impression you make which matters because you have to live with that image. What I am suggesting is that you take time to look at yourself, to reassess yourself, to decide whether or not your long-established and long-accepted ideas about the image you choose to project are doing the job they should.

What you are doing is putting dress, mannerisms and appearance on the agenda, recognizing their importance and then letting your ideas take their course. You are raising image to a conscious level so that when you buy clothes or get your hair done you have in the back of your mind the idea that you aren't just trying to please yourself. You are trying to achieve a positive effect and using dress as a weapon against your shyness, and that is something we will do again in the course of this book. Being shy, and doing something constructive about it, may well even put you in a better position than someone who isn't shy enough to try to help himself or herself. You aren't just overcoming shyness, you are getting ahead of the field simply by thinking constructively about the problem, so there is hope.

Other important factors

It isn't just dress sense we are talking about when we think about image. Dress is just part of it, and it isn't the most important part. I have spent time talking about it because it is something which we can change relatively easily, and from which we can get instant results, but there are other things. When I was much younger a girl used to walk past my house every day. She was an attractive girl and I used to wish she wasn't so shy. She would walk with her head down avoiding people's eyes, her shoulders rounded and back stooped so that every fibre of her being proclaimed her shyness. She went away from home for a while and when she came back she was different. She walked with her head up and her shoulders back with her hair loose about her face. She smiled as she walked and everything about her proclaimed confidence. It was a startling transformation.

In this girl's case, it wasn't a change of clothes, it was a change of manner. She had acquired confidence in some other way I was never to discover, but she was certainly different, and that difference was a huge improvement. No doubt her confidence came from within, but it works both ways. Learning to consciously project that image can do nothing but improve confidence and reduce shyness.

Posture

So projecting an image is more than just dressing differently. It is just as much about posture, about the way we walk and even the amount we smile. Indeed these other factors may be *more* important than mere clothes, but the right clothes can be a stimulus to developing a more

upright posture, to standing with our head up and our
shoulders back. We have been talking about clothes and
dressing just because it is something we can do relatively
easily. You could buy a new dress and go out for the
evening and create an entirely new image by doing that and
nothing else. Learning to stand and walk more assertively
takes longer, and just how do you do it?

You can do a certain amount just by becoming aware of
the way you look, by using that mirror. You can try to stand
better, to walk better and you can even practise smiling at
yourself. You can experiment with your appearance using
clothes as well as posture. Another way to do it is to take
up a sporting activity, if you aren't already doing that. If you
are physically fit you feel good and you look good. A little
narcissism does no harm. If you go to keep fit classes you
become aware of your body, and you may become aware
of just how terrible it looks so that you will do something
about it. If you feel good you will look good and that will
make you less shy.

I know someone who went on holiday and found that
there was a naturist beach close to his hotel. He had always
been rather shy about his body and would never have
imagined himself going naked on a public beach, but on
this holiday it seemed to be the natural and accepted thing
to do and his friends thought nothing about it, so he took
advantage of the opportunity even though he was very nervous about it. It turned out to be a very enlightening experience. Other people took naturism for granted and probably
did it every summer, but for this shy and rather inhibited
person it was a liberation. In discarding his clothes he actually seemed to discard his inhibitions. The change that he
had made in his mode of dress was extreme—he simply
abandoned his clothes. On the beach he felt fitter, more
confident and less shy. Everyone on the beach was there on
exactly the same terms, expressing the same image of
relaxed enjoyment without inhibitions.

I would not recommend this experience to everyone, but
it does illustrate the point that you can change the way you
feel by changing some of the mannerisms or clothes or
demeanour or whatever you have come to accept as being

an essential part of you. Do it by yourself, do it using a mirror or any other aid you can, but do it.

Where can you get a new image from?

Girls

Anyone in the dress designing business or the image making business has to get their ideas from somewhere. They start with an idea which is borrowed from somewhere, but after much thought it evolves into something of their own. No one can pluck an idea completely out of the air, and the same is true for you. Look around and see what other women are wearing and how they look. You might like the style of someone you know, or you might like the image of someone you see in a magazine. It doesn't matter where the original idea comes from—in the end it will be your own style.

It will help you to create a new image if you know what sort of image you are trying to create, so for those who don't have a great interest in clothes it is worthwhile getting back to pencil and paper. You can't start sketching clothes unless you have a particular talent for that, but you can write in words the sort of person you are, and the sort of image that person might want to present. If you can establish that in your mind, common sense will guide your dress sense.

What about boys?

You may have noticed that these remarks are more relevant to girls than to boys, because even in this day and age boys have fewer options in dress. Older people too will not find changing their image all that easy, yet there is more to image than just appearance or looks. That is quite clear, and sex appeal for example is elusive and hard to define. So is charisma or star quality, something which we can all recognize. What are these things and how does someone achieve them? Somehow appearance is only part of it, and the rest may be to do with confidence and demeanour. Yet how are these things transmitted if not by our image? You don't go up to a girl and say: 'Talk to me, I'm confident.' Such impressions are transmitted more subtly.

In later chapters we will talk about how we can achieve a relaxed demeanour, and how we can develop our social skills, but for now try to develop the concept of image, because if it's in your mind, then you're working on it. Shoes, ties, casual wear, all these things make an impression before you say a word. Value yourself and say it in your clothes.

A boy I once knew was very successful with girls. He seemed to be a shy individual with little to say for himself, but whilst the rest of his contemporaries were floundering, he always got the girl and no one ever worked out how he did it. He appeared to make no effort, rarely spoke to girls at social events, and relied entirely on his image. He dressed formally and expensively, and in that he projected a more mature image than his friends. He also had an E-Type Jaguar, the ultimate image maker. Yet the girls he met at parties didn't know that he had a sports car outside—but he knew.

Don't rush out and buy a sports car—you don't need to. The lesson that you really need to learn is that if you look relaxed and comfortable, if you know that you are appropriately and well dressed in the way that you think suits you, an E-Type Jaguar becomes a mere affectation. You need the psychological equivalent of an E-Type, and that is what we are in the process of organizing, so you must start to take trouble with the things that you haven't, till now, thought to be important.

Getting down to it

It may seem facile to imagine that you can simply adjust your image and change your life, but that isn't what I'm suggesting. All I'm saying is that you have to make a start, make a statement, do something, and making a change in your image even by buying an item of clothing is doing just that. You simply have to do it, you have to make a start if you're going to overcome your shyness.

You have to make a start and you have to get on with it. It may seem daft to stand in front of a mirror and talk to yourself, smile at yourself and practise standing straighter, but what else are you going to do? You won't get rid of your shyness by just wishing it away. No doubt you've already tried that, and it doesn't work. No, you have to actually *do* something, do something positive and experiment a bit, and that takes effort, and it takes a little courage. It's worth all the effort because your shyness is a major disability and because it is something you can overcome. You owe it to yourself to get on with it.

Moving on

Well, we have made a start. We have done something, however small, even if all we have done is to buy a new tie or a new sweater. We are on the move. We have put our shoulder to the great monolith of our shyness and moved it just a bit. That first move is an important one because it shows us that we can do something about our shyness, and if we can do just a little now, think how much we will be able to do in the future.

REMEMBER:

- You can't get rid of your shyness by wishing it away. You have to do something.
- Everyone projects an image. It is possible to make that image more positive by making a few simple changes.
- If you improve your image so that you look good, you will also feel good.
- Feeling good improves your confidence and reduces your shyness.

Chapter 5

Improving your performance

Improving your performance means improving the way you manage the various situations you have to face in your everyday life. The situations may appear very different from each other, but in some major ways they are similar and there are some general rules which you can learn which will help you to manage this part of your life.

Later in the book we will look at some specific situations which are different from the usual, but for now let's look at the way we manage our day-to-day lives. Shyness is about the way we manage relationships, from the most casual exchange with a stranger in the street to the most intimate of our encounters. Shyness is about people, what we say to them, how we look at them, how we feel about them and most of all, what we feel about ourselves. It is also very much about what we think people feel about us, because shy people are very aware of the effect they have on others. Dealing with our shyness is all about changing the way we manage these encounters with other people.

We have dealt at length with one aspect of this phenomenon, that being how we look to other people, what our first impression is going to be like, what our image is going to be like. We have to move on now, just as you have to move on in a relationship, however brief. After we have made our first impression we have to talk, look, smile, move and think. These things constitute a performance, a performance of ourselves. We have to act out ourselves for the person we are relating to.

What do we mean by performance?

By performance we mean the way we act, but this acting has nothing to do with drama or the stage and everything to do with the way we behave when we are with our friends, or if we are in public places with other people. Everyone performs, whether they are aware of it or not, and some people do it well whilst others do it badly. Shy people find this kind of public performance more difficult than most other people do.

There's nothing false about performance, no artifice, nothing contrived, and that's the way it should be. We should all be doing what comes naturally because if we try to fake our public performance it shows, and other people don't like the feeling that they are being conned. That's the way it should be, but of course we all alter our performance according to the company we are in, and most of us make this adjustment naturally without being aware of it—it's just part of the normal social intercourse we have with others. That isn't the same as giving a contrived performance to impress someone, it isn't putting on an act, it's acting naturally.

If you aren't good at this, if you're self-conscious and therefore aware that your performance isn't as good as other people's, you have a problem. The worse your performance is, the more gauche you may appear to be, the more shy you will appear and if you appear shy, you will feel shy. It just goes round and round. If, on the other hand, your performance is polished and competent, you will feel confident and your shyness will disappear in time.

A natural progression

Improving your performance is a natural progression from your efforts to improve your image. Good performance begins with the knowledge that we look confident and relaxed. Like so many other things, it's all a matter of building on what has already been achieved, of taking a few small steps at a time, preferably in the right direction.

You might assume that a satisfactory public performance should come naturally, but that isn't always the case. Some people are good at it, and some people aren't. For some people it is a skill to be acquired, or rather a set of skills—our social skills. Take an example, meeting someone's eyes. That seems fairly straightforward. When you are talking to someone you look into their eyes. But do you? Do you look into their eyes all the time, or do you look into them and then look away? If you look into them and look away, how much do you look at them and how much do you look away?

What we actually do during a conversation is to look into the other person's eyes and then look away again. That's what everyone does, but the problem is that if you look at them too much you tend to appear aggressive and you make them uncomfortable. Look too little and you run the risk of seeming to be uninterested. Some people do this just right and they do it naturally so that they never even think about it, but for some shy people there is the risk of embarrassment, and they are aware of that risk and are self-conscious in the literal sense. Or perhaps they may be doing it wrong without being aware of it. They may be looking just a little too much, or just a little too little, and although the person they are talking to won't really know why, he or she will be aware of being slightly ill at ease in their company. Meeting someone's eyes just the right amount is a social skill, and like any skill, it is something which can be learned.

Social skills

What are these skills we have to learn? You haven't been aware of them up until now, so why are they so important all of a sudden? They are important only because you have decided to do something about your shyness and you have to look at all areas where you can make an impact on it. You want to make changes in the way you interact with others, and looking at the way you make these interactions now is a first step. There are all sorts of social skills, and you could make a list yourself. I can remember meeting an old friend after not having seen him for many years. To my surprise he shook me warmly by the hand. I had never shaken his hand before—we had never needed to. He had been away and started a new life, and in his new lifestyle the rules had changed. It was entirely normal for him to shake hands with anyone he met. I was suddenly aware of the differences which had developed between us. I was aware of the importance of a simple thing like shaking hands. I had discovered that he had a social skill which I didn't have, and as a result I would have seemed as out of place with his new friends as he now did with his old friends.

When you meet someone do you shake their hand? Do you shake the hand of everyone you meet? Whose hand do you shake and whose do you not shake? If you had to work this sort of thing out from first principles every time you would get nowhere, particularly as the rules are different in different societies and in different parts of the world. It is something you should do naturally without any thought at all, and you probably do most of the time. Just the same, it might be worth thinking about your responses. The same is true for many other small but important social skills.

Feeling awkward

If you are shy you may feel awkward in some social situations, anything from a small gathering to a lively party. It isn't very pleasant, and feeling awkward makes you feel shy. Why do you feel awkward? I don't mean that you should go back into your childhood to find reasons, I mean what is making you feel awkward right now? It may be that you are sweating or that your tummy is churning, and we will talk about that later, but it might be because you are uncertain about how you should be responding. Should you smile, should you shake hands, should you use first names or a more formal type of address, should you sit down or stand up? Using your social skills may be a problem for you, and you might be able to do better.

There is a whole repertoire of social exchanges which have nothing to do with the normal use of speech, which is for exchanging ideas. This repertoire is to do with exchanging information about yourself, about who you are, what you're feeling like, whether you have time to talk, and also whether you want to explore the possibility of developing a relationship. That information is also contained in the way we dress and present ourselves—our image, and in the gestures we use. It is to do with the amount of eye contact we make, whether we smile or frown, all sorts of non-verbal things. If we are shy, we tell people that too.

I am not suggesting in all this that you try to hide the fact that you are shy. We should be ourselves, but if we understand the mechanisms of our social intercourse and can improve our performance, we can gain control of our lives and actually convey the messages we want to convey. We can in this way overcome our shyness because we will know that we are in control. That is the only comfortable way to be. How do we gain this control?

Gaining control of our social exchanges

Social exchanges occur all the time, any time in fact that we meet another person, pass another person in the street or if we make a speech or address a meeting. They can be businesslike and formal, or they can be intimate and personal. The way we manage these exchanges involves our image, our non-verbal communication, and the content of the messages we transmit. Shy people aren't necessarily bad at all of these elements of communication, but they tend not to perform too well across the board because shyness affects most aspects of our personality. Being aware that we communicate badly in turn makes our shyness worse, so we go round and round. Poor communication is the part of our shyness which causes most anguish. Not only are these encounters difficult, the anticipation of them is nerve-wracking so that we begin to dread going to a party, or going to a business lunch or to a meeting where we may have to contribute something. If we could gain control of these exchanges so that we begin to feel comfortable in social situations, we will soon feel less shy.

We have made a declaration of our intent to work towards this end by working on our image, so that in a passive way we have changed our non-verbal statement. We are simply saying something different about ourselves by changing the way we look. Now we must do something more positive and active, we have to improve our social skills. That seems a difficult concept at first, so how do we go about it?

As in all of our discussions, the first thing to do is to define the problem. Just what are the situations which give us problems, and what problems do they give us? We need a little detective work, and it will come as no surprise to learn that we will need our diary to help us. We have to decide not just what situations give us problems, but which problems are the most difficult, and which are the ones we can tackle with the minimum of difficulty. We have to make a start, and it is essential to take on the easier problems first.

At the moment our shyness has no form, it's just an amorphous mass of embarrassment and discomfort. We have to give it form, pin it down, and then dissect it, removing first the parts which can be reached easily, and then working up to the more difficult areas. We cannot simply reduce shyness to that series of problems we have with social encounters, but these problems are part of our shyness and they are a part we can reach and deal with, so that is what we will do. Get out the diary and start to make notes about your day-to-day encounters. A young man might make notes such as these:

Saturday: Shopping today. Don't like shopping on a Saturday as shops are so busy. Always feel like a shoplifter. Pass Mr Jones in Main Street. One of those situations where I see him from a distance and don't know whether to look him in the eye or not, or what to say. Eventually nod to him but he says 'Hello.' He must think I'm a wally. Quiet afternoon, but apprehensive about Jimmy's party as I hate parties.

Evening: Meet Paul and Derek in the Coachman for a drink before the party. Arrive late. Apprehensive about actually going in. Who will be there and who will I have to talk to? Fortunately the two just march in and greet everyone

like long lost friends. I spot Martin, thank goodness.
Everyone in good form, but I really don't know many people. Talk to Martin, but can't keep up with Paul and Derek
who are dancing with girls they've never seen before. They
can just walk up to people and talk to them. Feel conspicuous. Talk to some people I don't know. Don't really know
what to talk about. Probably shy like me, or they would be
dancing too. See Jane who I fancy but fail again. Just
haven't got the chat. Why can't girls see that it's just shyness
and I am not really a wally?

Sunday: Quiet day. Read papers. Long walk.

Monday: Work again. Our busy period. Boss comes in to
thank me for last week in front of everyone. Very embarrassing as I don't know what to say. Just mutter 'It was
nothing.' Lunchtime—have to take broken pen back to
shop. Queue at counter so leave it till a quieter time. Lunch
by myself in Burger Place. Hate eating alone.....

....and so on.

So this young man has problems. The point of keeping
this diary was so that he could identify his problems and
start to solve them. The first thing he had to do was to
make as exhaustive a list as possible of these problems,
from the smallest to the largest. This was his list:

- Feeling uncomfortable in shops.
- Meeting the eye of someone in the street. Knowing
  what to say.
- Apprehensive before party.
- Arriving at party.
- Meeting new people at party. Knowing what to say.
- Embarrassed talking to girls.
- Embarrassed by praise in front of others.
- Unhappy about complaining about faulty goods.
- Eating in public. Where do you look?

So our friend has his list, or rather the start of a list because
he will want to add to it as time goes on. His list should be
as specific as possible and as detailed as possible, because
this list is the enemy. It is the thing which has to be overcome, and it is important to identify and to know your

enemy. When you have sorted out the problems with your performance, what do you do about them?

Making a start

You can't change the world overnight, but you can make a start to overcoming your problems. The trouble is, with so many little problems where do you start? It might be best to chose one or two things which you find difficult and start with those. Make sure that they aren't too complicated, and in particular make sure that they are things which you meet often and can practise frequently.

Look at your chosen problem areas in the greatest detail you can, preferably when you next meet that problem. Let's choose talking to strangers. There are several things here, who you talk to, how you start a conversation, what you talk about, and how you finish the conversation. That is the content of the conversation. Then there are the non-verbals. Do you meet their eyes, and if so how frequently? How close do you stand to them? Do you have any unfortunate mannerisms? You really need to go into the greatest possible detail. Write down everything you can about a particular problem, from as many angles as possible, and then decide what you're going to do about them.

Dealing with your problems

It would be nice if you had an expert, some great authority, standing by your elbow, whispering in your ear telling you what you should do and what you shouldn't do. It would be nice, but you haven't got that, and it wouldn't work anyway. Perhaps you could get a book which would tell you how to deal with all of these problems. You can't, and if you could it wouldn't work. These things wouldn't work because we are all different, and what would work for someone else mightn't work for you. And then these things are different for different parts of the world and for different social situations. There is only one person who can decide what you have to do, and how you have to go about things. That person is you.

So how do you improve your own performance? How can you analyse the way you behave? It isn't as difficult as you might think. Some of the improvement happens by itself simply because you have become aware of the situation. If you keep a diary and make a note of the things which contribute to your poor performance, you will automatically improve on it. The more detailed your record, the more you are able to correct the small things which together make for poor performance and which make you uncomfortable. As before, simply by being aware you will have made a start. Then you have to build on that start.

What tools can you use? If you had a video of every social transaction you had in a given day your mistakes, if that is the word, would be perfectly obvious and you would rapidly learn. That's how sportspeople learn, and how public speakers and salespeople learn. You can't have a video camera running all the time to give you an objective view, but you do have a camera running inside your head giving you some sort of impression, albeit a subjective one. To get another angle you have to use your imagination, and a mirror or a video camera if you happen to have access to one, and something most of us have, a cassette tape recorder. The most important of these is your imagination.

When you have identified the things you are doing badly you have to practise them. You can do this privately at home, and you must do it. There is no time for that other enemy, embarrassment, and no time for not having time. Overcoming shyness is a major commitment so you have to make time. You may not like talking to yourself, but you have to do it.

The first thing you have to do is to sit down with your diary and work out for yourself what you may be doing wrong. Most people have a good idea about their shortcomings, but write them down, and write down how you can improve on them. Then you must practise. Relive situations which have not gone the way you would have liked, watching yourself in the mirror, and listening to yourself on a tape if it is a problem with what you say or the way you say it. It's just like improving your image, but this time it's a moving, speaking image. One tip which might help: imagine that you are someone else watching, someone whose opinion you would value. If you are a girl meant to be talking to a boy, imagine what the boy would make of your performance. Put yourself in their position. Most shy people have a good imagination, so you may be surprised at just how realistic your private performance can appear. If you get flustered in the real situation, you will get flustered at home, so practice isn't that difficult.

Getting on with it

Let's use the example of the young man we talked about earlier, and his problem with eye contact, which is something he wrote about in his diary. It wasn't something he had spent a lot of time thinking about before, but now he was concentrating on it, first by himself and later in real-life situations. Just what did he look like to other people when he was talking to them? Did he look aggressive or did he look uninterested? The only way to find out was for him to talk to himself in the mirror, to look and look away, to practise normal conversation. He had to do this until he was confident that he had got it about right, so that he would sound and look confident. He had to be like any actor and produce a competent performance.

He could do the same thing with his problem about meeting people in the street. Should he meet their eyes one hundred yards away, or fifty yards, and should he speak to them, or nod, or smile? He had to work out on paper what he thought was the best thing to do—best for himself, that is. Then he had to experiment at home with a mirror, just to see what he looked like. When he thought he had got it right he had to practise, to rehearse until he could do it automatically.

If you feel any embarrassment or reluctance about practising these things, try and put it out of your mind. What do you think they do at sales courses where brash young men and women are taught how to sell themselves, which is the first step in selling a product? There is always a video camera there, and the group studies the things we have been talking about. They learn special selling techniques which help them when they meet a customer and have to engage his attention long enough to sell him something. They cannot afford to intimidate or embarrass a client, so they practise something which all of us, and particularly shy people, find difficult. How do they do it?

A sales rep will usually bring a folder with him when he goes to see a client. Why? Is it because it contains special information which the client is expected to read? It could probably contain a page of the telephone directory because its function is to get over the problem of eye contact. The rep doesn't want to be sitting opposite his client looking into his eyes, or making the client look into his eyes with all the potential for embarrassment that holds. So both client and rep look at the folder. The folder facilitates the social encounter.

People watching

How can you decide what is appropriate in any given situation? It's all very well to say that you have to find your own way, to sort out what suits you, but there is more to it than that. It is very hard to get an objective view of one's own behaviour and to decide what is right and what is wrong. You have to find some guidelines which will help you to improve your public performance, and one way of doing this is to watch someone else.

It would be quite wrong to try to copy someone else because the result would not be true for you, but you can see how other people do it. You don't have to copy exactly what they do, but as in the matter of creating an image, you can get ideas which you can then make your own. If you are going to see how someone else does it, choose someone who does it well and watch them. Dealing with your shyness is now becoming a major task, something that you are learning to do subconsciously all of the time, and very deliberately at least part of the time.

You have raised to the level of consciousness things that you have always taken for granted before, so when you next go to a party or similar event, try not to be completely preoccupied with your own shyness. Take time to watch how other people make their entrance. Do they look shy, or do they look brash, and what are they really thinking and feeling? Are they covering up, which they may well be doing, and if they are, how do they do it? You have embarked on a learning experience, so open your mind and let ideas come in. You may well decide that other people find some things as difficult as you do, but they have learned better ways of dealing with them than you have. Arriving at a party or at a public event is difficult for everyone, so it is an interesting thing to watch.

Arriving

People use all sorts of methods to manage difficult situations, and you will do the same. It might just be possible for you to change your method to something which is more successful. You don't have to march in, blustering and shouting, but you might want to try to arrive quietly, pick out someone you know, and have a standard opening gambit or gambits to get you over that most difficult few minutes when you feel strange and uncertain. You can do the same when you are introduced to someone for the first time. Everyone is flustered at that moment, so you have to have thought out a way of dealing with that problem in advance.

Being a host

Being a host or a hostess is another area which people manage very differently. Someone who is used to being a host for business reasons is well worth watching. He or she will have done a little homework and will know who is coming, how they are to be seated, if applicable, and so on. No matter where the meal or the event is, a good host will act as a master of ceremonies. He or she will be able to put people at their ease, to deal with the uncertainty they feel when they first arrive, make introductions, offer a drink and manage the conversation.

Someone who may be shy, or who has no experience of managing these situations, relies on the guests to get themselves organized and the evening may go well or it may not. There is no effort to put people at their ease, or rather that person may lack the skill to do that. Being a host is a skill which can be taught and learned, and you can learn it simply by watching. Next time you are at such an event, watch the expert.

You can't simply copy an expert, but you can get a few tips. You can learn the value of preparation, and the advantage to taking control of the situation. If you are really shy this may well be the sort of thing that you find difficult, and it is the sort of thing which you can improve by watching, learning and practising. If you are due to be a host or hostess, prepare well and rehearse at home. You don't have to feel silly—you can be sure that is exactly what the host you have been watching will have done in advance. His performance was rehearsed and polished.

In many areas a shy person is simply not doing the things that other people have the confidence to do. It does take confidence to stand up at home with a tape recorder or a mirror and practise something which you think others take for granted—but then you don't know what other people do, so forget about them. Have the confidence to do whatever you have to do in any situation to make it easier for you.

Now is the time to start identifying other problem areas, if possible with the use of a diary or of notes, and then work out strategies for dealing with them. There will be much more about this in the next chapter.

REMEMBER:

- Make a list of the things you find difficult.
- Decide how you might be able to improve them.
- Be prepared to practise by yourself first using a mirror and a tape recorder, and later in company.
- You can improve your social skills and learn new ones.
- Study and practise things you find difficult.

Chapter 6

Managing situations

Whilst we are still thinking about improving the way we do things, there is one important point to remember. Your ability to do things with more confidence will improve quite quickly, but your feeling of shyness, that mental awareness of being a shy person, will take longer to go away. It didn't come overnight, and it certainly won't go away overnight, but you have to believe that it will eventually diminish to a point where you won't have to worry about it.

For the moment we are continuing the same theme, basically saying that if we are more socially competent, if we feel ourselves to be more socially competent, and if we appear to other people to be more socially competent, we will feel more comfortable in social situations, more relaxed, and we will *be* more confident. Then our shyness becomes less of an impediment to the enjoyment of our lives, and with our increased competence comes a decrease in our shyness. We can talk later about changing our attitudes, and about increasing the scope of our lives. This is the payoff for the efforts we make now. In the longer term we would hope to expand our lives and so increase our sense of fulfilment. There is a great deal to play for.

Start with the familiar

Everyone is anxious to press ahead and make as much progress as possible, but if you try too hard you will be disappointed. You have to take things one step at a time, and you have to be satisfied that you are making progress in the area of your activity you are currently working on before taking on more, so don't be too ambitious. It is also worth saying that you have to keep at it. Progress is slow, sometimes painfully slow, and it is easy to become disillusioned. That is why it would be useful to have a counsellor to advise you—the main task of any counsellor is to keep you working, to set you goals and to give you encouragement. Unfortunately, it isn't easy to find a counsellor who deals with such things as shyness, so you'll just have to manage with my advice and encouragement, and with your own determination.

You have to work by looking at the more familiar things in your life and finding more successful ways of managing them. You have to keep at it, work in a methodical way and be satisfied with slow progress. If your shyness is worse in one particular area of your life you may be tempted to skip on to a discussion of the management of those more difficult aspects of your life, but that would be self-defeating. You can't separate out one area and ignore the rest, so take your time.

Just being aware of the problem may be one of the most important factors in overcoming your shyness. You are certainly aware that you are shy, but you've probably never spent time working out exactly what that means in terms of your everyday life, so stay with the familiar aspects of your life and study the way your shyness affects them, and how you can improve them, and only after you have become accustomed to always taking a critical look at your performance in any situation can you move on to other newer situations. You have to be self-aware and self-critical of your performance all the time, and when things don't go as well as expected you have to be prepared to work out why, and then decide what you can do to improve things. It really is a long-term plan.

Be honest

There is absolutely no place for self-deception. You can deceive anyone you like, even yourself. Being honest may have some unpleasant consequences. You might have to face up to the fact that your performance is worse than you thought. You might have to face up to the fact that some people just don't like you, and even that there might be legitimate reasons why they don't like you. Your shyness might make you abrupt and unpleasant, and you must remember that people will take you at face value. If you are unpleasant to them they won't stop to wonder why, or to make excuses. They will simply take offence. More about that later.

Planning

Can we improve the way we manage certain situations in a way similar to that which we used to improve our performance, and for that matter to the way we used to improved our image? It's a matter of raising to the conscious level something which we now manage automatically (but badly), and which other people also manage without any thought. If we are doing it less well than we could, we have to give it some thought and try to find out why. It is another practical way of making the best of ourselves and by so doing improving our ability to manage a situation, improve our confidence, and as a result reduce our shyness. It is simply another thing that we can do, and as we can do it, we should do it.

At the moment we just go out to events, to our work, to parties and so on without too much thought. Perhaps it's now time for us to give these events our critical attention, analyse just how we manage them and then think about how we can improve them by a little foresight and planning. We are still trying simply to make the best of ourselves, not to make ourselves into something different. We have to maximize our assets, and we can do that with the help of a little planning.

How do you manage difficult situations now?

First of all, what is a difficult situation? For our purposes it is any situation in which you are aware of your shyness, and that can be anything from a bus journey, to a meeting with a stranger, to a party or a business meeting. It can also be a meeting with someone of the opposite sex, because shyness is perhaps most commonly associated with these sometimes testing encounters. We give these situations no prior constructive thought, and play them by ear. We can do better.

We do give some aspects of these meetings thought. We take some trouble over our dress, hopefully now more than before, and we tend not to do any more than that so that when we arrive somewhere we are immediately in uncharted waters, full of uncertainty. What would happen if we did a little research, and tried to anticipate events? Surely we could obtain some prior warning of any possible pitfalls, and we might just be able to do something about avoiding them.

As shy people it is helpful if we put a little more effort into our day-to-day lives than people who aren't shy. We need to do that if we are to compete with our rivals, or even our friends, on a level playing field. We have to provide a counterbalance to our shyness. We do that by putting in some extra effort. It's sometimes easier to understand things when we see how other people have managed their problems, so let's consider how a girl called Laura learned something about planning and preparing.

Laura

Laura had always been excruciatingly shy—isn't it odd how often adjectives used to describe shyness can also be associated with pain? Laura was very, very shy, so shy that she came to me for advice. She was able to discuss her problems, and she did make efforts to change the way she looked and the way she behaved in public, and her efforts were met with some success. She did change her image sufficiently for her to begin to feel that bit more confident. She felt that she looked and performed more competently, but she still felt shy.

Worse than that, sometimes when she woke in the morning she would feel apprehensive and uneasy, even before she got out of bed. It was only after some thought that she would realize that she had to go to a party that evening, or to a dance, or even to a concert. She was a student, and these items were constantly on her social calender. She would be invited to them on a regular basis, and she would go with a group of friends, all of whom seemed to enjoy them, and who weren't in the least shy.

Laura's misery would last all day, and her sense of apprehension would grow and grow until she arrived at her destination. Outside she would feel sick, and entry into a busy reception or even to an informal party was a nightmare. Once she was in there, her friends would get on with the business of enjoying themselves whilst she would stand in a corner or make awkward conversation with a friend or sometimes with a boy or someone she didn't know. Afterwards she would go home to her flat. Sometimes she would weep because of her inability to have normal social contact with others.

One by one Laura's friends got themselves boyfriends and she had less and less company when she went out, so that she felt a greater need to be able to communicate with other people in a casual way. She was becoming desperate, and was very anxious to overcome her shyness. She just didn't know how to go about it. She had been working on her problem, but what could she do next?

I suggested to her that every time she went to an event of any sort, it was as if she was going for the first time. She felt the same sort of apprehension, and she didn't know why. It was something which came from within and she had never really asked herself why it happened. She didn't know which events were most difficult for her or, more importantly, why some events were more difficult than others. It was time she did some thinking. Was it the type of event? Was it the people who would be there? Was it her uncertainty about how she should act or how she should appear? Her basic problem seemed to be that she didn't trust herself to be natural, to respond to the approach of others in a matter-of-fact way because she had no confidence, and this lack of confidence made her uncertain in so many situations. She didn't know how she should behave or how she should respond, and the type of event she was going to attend affected the amount of apprehension she would feel. If it was to be a party, where girls were expected to meet boys and there was the possibility, however slight, of a physical relationship, she was really apprehensive. If her ability and competence were at stake, as in a tutorial or meeting, she was also apprehensive.

Laura discovered all this by analysing the way she had felt before and during recent events she had attended. She kept a note of how she felt and why, that is to say, who made her feel shy, what events made her feel shy and, if possible, why they made her feel that way. Finally she tried to make a list of what she could do to make these events less traumatic. It was all part of an exercise to raise these vague ideas of unease and shyness into a level of conscious awareness so that her shyness took on some kind of form.

Doing something about it

What could Laura, and what can you, do to anticipate these difficult events, plan for these events, and by so doing make them less traumatic? Well, every time you go to an event it is like the first time because you haven't given it any constructive thought. If you are going somewhere, simply ask a few questions and find out all that you can about this party or meeting. Who is going to be there, how many people are going to be there, what sort of evening is it going to be? Find out about transport, particularly transport home, so that you have some control over the situation. Knowledge gives you power, so find out as much as you can.

A shy person isn't usually too good at improvising, so plan ahead. If you know the names of some of those attending you have a head start. If you are bad at names, make a list of people attending and learn their names so that when you meet them you can use their name. That always sounds confident and impressive, and if you can remember something about their interests that too is impressive. When did you last meet them? If you remember, or seem to remember, more about another person than they remember about you, you have an advantage and you certainly won't seem shy. This may seem a little artificial, but you are playing this game to win. Parties and meetings are full of 'game players', and you have to become competitive too.

If you want to know how these games work, just watch. It can be fascinating watching how other people behave in company. You are now in the business of overcoming shyness, and that is a major task which involves study. Remember that it was suggested that the next time you are at a party you should observe the antics of the arrivals. Some will bluster and create a fuss, some will be quiet and drift to the back of the crowd, some will head for the bar. It may be that the life-and-soul of the party is a shy person who has found a way of overcoming, or rather masking, his or her shyness. The point is that everyone finds arriving at an event difficult. It is hard to join a group which may already have formed an identity, and many not-so-shy people use a ploy to get them over that particular hurdle, and will use different ploys for different situations. You can do the same.

Gambits

Before you can plan ways of arriving at an event or of managing a situation you have to have some idea what you are going to say to people. You need to have a few conversational gambits, because that's what other people do. A friend of mine used to walk up to the first person he came to at an event and say 'Don't I know you from somewhere?' Of course he didn't, but a conversation would ensue in which the person would say 'I don't think so—unless I met you at...' By the time they had decided that they really didn't know each other at all they were friends for life. I was never able to decide whether my friend really thought that he already knew just about everyone he met or whether this was a conversational gambit. Starting a conversation with a question, no matter how banal, forces an answer, and a dialogue has begun.

You can improve on these conversational gambits, and it is useful if you have something to talk to people about. Making small talk is difficult for many people, but it is

something we have to do. You can't just walk up to someone and discuss the intimate details of your life. If you are
to interest someone in yourself, you have to be able to be
interesting and to make interesting conversation, and it
helps if you have a few set-pieces. If you are to use them,
you have to first invent them. You have to have something
you can walk up to a complete stranger and say. How
about, 'Do you know many people here?' And when they
answer you can say, 'I don't, I only know Ron and Phyllis. I
work with Ron you see. I'm.....'. There you are, you've
introduced yourself, you've explained who you are, and the
person you're talking to now feels the need to introduce
himself or herself too. If that person is also shy, they will be
delighted to be able to have such an easy relaxed conversation. If you've done some homework, you will know something about people present and you can talk about them.

Don't be reticent about asking questions. Most people
love to talk, but if you are going to encourage people to
talk you have to practise the art of listening. It's easy to
stand and let words go past you. If you want to impress
you have to look interested and actually listen so that you
can respond appropriately. Learn how to prime people,
learn how to compliment people. How do you acquire
these skills? You learn by experience, by actually doing
them. Nail someone at your next party and try an opening
gambit, and then try to keep the conversation going by listening and responding appropriately. Any opening gambit
will do. You could simply walk up to someone and say,
'Hello, I'm....' and take it from there.

Remember, conversation is an art. It's an art that can be
learned and practised, and when competence has been
achieved, confidence follows.

You can practise at any event you are attending, but you
can also practise at home, using a tape recorder. You don't
have to be crazy to talk to yourself, you can do it as a way
of practising your conversation, and you can practise in
your imagination in a car, or in bed, anywhere. Practise so
that you know what the sound of your own voice is like, so
that you are used to it and can be relaxed with it. Learn
how to avoid talking too much, or too little. Develop an ear

for your own conversation, listen to yourself and keep practising.

Slow down

One of the most common faults shy people have is a
tendency to speak before they think and to act before they
have considered the consequences. This is a simple physical
speeding up, a reaction to their shyness. A shy person will
become flustered, and will rush to fill a gap in the conversation with some comment, whether or not it is appropriate.
Often it won't be appropriate and may sound silly or worse,
rude. We have all had that experience.

If shy people seem clumsy it is often because they try to
do things too quickly. They may reach for a drink, knocking
over another glass in the process. If they are asked to
demonstrate something they will rush at it in order to avoid
embarrassment so that they haven't time to think before
they act. They may thus do the wrong thing when they
know what the right thing should be and thus seem silly,
the very thing they were trying to avoid by their haste.

Shy people should have the magic words 'Slow down'
permanently emblazoned before them. You may speed up
because you are flustered, but what does that really mean?
Being flustered means being embarrassed because you have
become conspicuous, perhaps having been made the centre
of attention by being asked a question at a meeting. Or a
pause may have developed in the conversation, and you
don't like pauses. Nobody does because a pause causes
embarrassment, the shuffling of feet and general unease.
Someone has to fill the vacuum, and often it is the shy person with a stupid remark made without thought. That is
something to be avoided.

How do you manage this desire to speed up, to jump in
to fill the gap, or to say the first thing that comes into your
head when you are asked a question? There is only one
answer—you have to slow down. You have to think before
you speak, think before you act. And the way you do that is
to go again down that by now well-trodden path, you have
to listen, you have to go home and practise, and you have

to put your practice into effect at every opportunity presents itself.

When you are next in a public situation, listen to yourself. How do you manage pauses? Do you think before you answer, or do you jump into gaps in the conversation to the detriment of your image? If you do, you have to do some homework. You can use a cassette recorder to help you, but you can just talk to yourself if you want to. Try a little conversation, and try leaving a pause without jumping in. What does a pause sound like? If you are to leave pauses in real-life conversations you have to know what they sound like, and you have to know that you can stay quiet and let someone else fill the gap.

Ask yourself a question...and allow time before you start your answer. Enjoy the pause. Ask a technical question, and instead of giving the first answer which comes into your head...stall. Say, 'Well...' and pause... 'I think the answer is...'. Learn to leave pauses, let them hang and don't get flustered.

Part of my job is teaching young doctors how to manage consultations, and one of the things I have to teach them is the use of the pause. When a doctor is talking to a patient there is the tendency to fill in gaps in the conversation. If a doctor wants to get more information from a patient he can do that by leaving a pause after the patient has finished his or her answer and letting it hang until the patient *has* to say something. By using this technique a doctor can almost force the patient to say more than he otherwise would, or might want to—for example, information about a drinking problem or marital difficulties which the doctor feels is relevant in the treatment of the patient and should be discussed.

It is a common technique: just watch a TV interviewer extract information from an unwary interviewee. I have heard an interviewer say that he could make any interviewee cry 'on camera' whenever he wanted, just by asking the right question and leaving the pause. It illustrates the power of the pause. It is as important in conversation, if not more powerful, than any spoken word. You should make friends with the pause, and if you don't use it at least don't be frightened of it. Practise dealing with it, practise having it as part of your conversational gambits, and if you really want to put pressure on someone at a meeting, try your pause. It is a powerful tool which can have startling and gratifying results.

Slow down your talking. Slow your delivery. Practise talking slowly using your cassette player or when you are in the car on your own. A slow deliberate delivery is more impressive than a gabbled reply. If you speak slowly and quietly you will be taken as being wise and sensible, whether this is true or not. It's all to do with practice and experiment at home, and practice in the real situation when you are proficient.

The reflected question

When you get the hang of studying and using conversation, there are other conversational ploys you can use. When I am teaching young doctors consultation techniques, I always include the use of the reflected question. This can be very helpful, like the use of the pause, in persuading other people to do the talking. It is also useful in difficult situations when you are asked a question and you aren't sure of the answer. If you don't want to give a direct answer to a question, simply pause and say, 'What do *you* think?' If someone says 'Why don't you do so-and-so,' you can answer, 'Why do you think I should?' You are reflecting the question back to the person who has asked it, and nine times out of ten the questioner will be only too delighted to give his or her own opinion, thus letting you off the hook. Again, try to practise the use of the reflected question. It can be fascinating watching how these conversational gambits work in real situations.

Managing conversations

Conversations are very interesting, they are important and if you study them you can develop conversational skills. Look at conversations critically and see how they work. Notice that most people who ask questions aren't really interested in your answer. They are usually more interested in preparing their response, or in telling you what they think. An interviewer has to actually be taught to listen to the answer he is given to a question so that he doesn't ask a subsequent question which has already been answered. People don't listen, and often they don't look, and their mind may be on something else altogether. If you want to engage their attention of course you can, perhaps by saying something personal, controversial or outrageous, but a lot of conversation is just intellectual wallpaper, a form of social intercourse. You can use it to your advantage, and of course you can stop someone else from using it to their advantage. Learn and practise the tricks of the trade.

Managing events

Let's go back to that problem of just how you manage events. How do you manage your arrival at a party? How do you manage arriving at a dinner party, or a small social gathering? How do you manage meeting someone, or going on a date? The chances are you have no idea how you do these things. You have no plans, haven't thought how you are going to do it. At least you are now developing the art of conversation, but you have to practise these difficult events too. The only way to do that is in your imagination, just by thinking your way through a difficult event.

Make a plan. Think how you would manage a situation if you weren't shy. If you were a confident person, what would you do differently? Say you are a boy going on a date, what can you do to make yourself seem a little more confident? You might bring flowers, but that would be over the top and might cause embarrassment, but if it is a dance you are going to, a corsage might be nice, in a colour which wouldn't clash with the girl's dress, of course! Even a box of chocolates can impress, provided the girl isn't on a diet. If you are going to do something like that, don't be half-hearted. You need confidence, or at least a confident air, and you know how to achieve that.

If you are a girl, even in this enlightened age, your social role tends to be more passive so that you are more likely to be in receipt of the present rather than the donor. Just the same, receiving a gift or a compliment can be as difficult as giving one. Of course you appreciate the gesture, even if it's the last thing you want. In all things, there is nothing which impresses like enthusiasm unless it's humour. Humour is more difficult to manage, but you can be enthusiastic about the efforts of your partner. You shouldn't be afraid to manage social situations, particularly if your partner for the evening isn't very good at it.

You should have that skill. You should have done some research so that you know what sort of event it is you're going to, and who may be there. You will know who you're going with, and how they will react. Remember that you have worked on your image so that the first impression you make on entering will be the one you want to make. If you say nothing, other people may have noticed you and be impressed, but decide in advance how you are going to proceed. Are you going to find someone to talk to? Are you going to sit quietly? When you are flustered, as everyone is when they arrive somewhere new, you tend to either be on auto-pilot and have little control over what is happening, or else you may talk too much. That is why thinking things through, practising in your mind and working to a plan can help you to get started. Once you have relaxed things are easier. Still, there is always the potential for disaster.

Disaster planning

Yes, for the shy person, for the weary or the unprepared, disaster lurks round every corner. What kind of disaster? Well, how about opening your mouth to put your foot in it? How about inadvertently insulting someone? Or spilling your drink down your dress, or worse, someone else's dress, or arriving in the same dress as someone else—the list is endless. You'll know them all.

Some disasters can be spectacular. A friend of mine was giving a speech after a dinner one night. He made a joke, not a very good joke, about another nationality. Someone

from that country took offence and began to shout, and
eventually had to be ushered, protesting loudly, from the
dining room by his friends. It is so easy to make the same
mistake in ordinary conversation. Sometimes it is difficult to
avoid, but there is no point in letting it prey on your mind
afterwards. It happens to all of us. You have to learn to survive disasters.

The best way is to ignore unpleasant occurrences. If you
say the wrong thing, or do the wrong thing, and you
respond by flapping, everyone is embarrassed. If you take it
in your stride, so will everyone else. You are the key figure
in managing your own disasters, so when disaster strikes
stay calm, if necessary ignore it, smile and try to put others
at their ease. How do you achieve all this? By practice. You
can practise disaster management by yourself, as always in
your imagination. If you know that you can manage a disaster, you lose your fear of disasters, and your confidence will
grow as your shyness diminishes. You are on the right
track.

So you are moving along the right lines, starting with the
way you look, the impression you make, and going on to
consider seriously what you say to people, and how you
manage difficult situations. It's all to do with building confidence which is a sure enemy of shyness. We will go on to
consider something slightly different. We will be looking at
the way we manage our internal environment, the way we
feel.

REMEMBER:

- Find out as much as you can about the event you
  are going to.
- Practise the things you find difficult in your imagi-
  nation, and that includes the art of conversation.
- Have a few conversational gambits at your disposal.
- Learn how to survive disasters.

Chapter 7

The physical side of shyness

It is impossible to separate the psychological side of any condition from its physical manifestations because our bodies and our minds are intimately related. Almost anything that we think or feel is reflected in some physical sensation. Think of the polygraph, or lie detector, which is used and trusted in the USA as a way of demonstrating when someone is telling a lie. There's nothing magic about this machine: it is simply a device which measures several physiological functions at the same time. It measures the heart rate and the rate of respiration, and it also measures something else.

Electrodes are placed on two of the fingers of the subject and the electrical resistance between them is measured. Any changes in this resistance are shown on a graph along with the other traces, so that changes in any of these functions are immediately demonstrated. The investigator asks routine questions, and when he asks a question directly regarding whatever it is that the subject is being questioned about, the trace is scrutinized very carefully for any deviations. If the subject tells a lie there is an immediate change in the traces on the graph, and the needles swing upwards indicating physiological stress.

There will be a change in the subject's breathing and heart rate, but the most dramatic change is in the electrical resistance between the finger electrodes. What is being measured? The resistance between the electrodes depends on the moisture on the skin, so it is really a measure of how much the subject is sweating. The surprising thing is just how immediate this response is. The split second that the subject tells a lie, the machine responds. It puts a whole new complexion on the 'sweaty hand' phenomenon. When you are stressed your pores open up instantaneously and you sweat, and even the slight stress of telling a lie can produce this result. Think of the different things that can happen to a shy person, think of the many stressful occurrences which can and do happen at a party or a meeting. Think of the way your body may be reacting throughout the evening.

Physical (or physiological) reactions

This physiological rollercoaster isn't confined to shy people: it happens to everyone. It is caused by the autonomic (i.e. automatic) part of our nervous system reacting to the stimulae it receives, so that if you are hot you sweat, if you are cold you shiver. It also reacts to internal, psychological stimulae such as fear or embarrassment. A shy or embarrassed person might blush in a stressful moment, and this response is immediate, and it is outwith the control of the subject. So many of the things our bodies do happen without us having anything control over them, and of course this is necessary. If we had to think about all the actions of our body we would have to focus our eyes the way we focus a camera, turn our sweat glands on and off, adjust the tone in our muscles so that we can stand and walk, arrange for our intestines to contract in a systematic way, and so on and so forth.

All of these reactions are necessary. They have a purpose and we couldn't live without them. Sometimes we wish they were a bit less intrusive. We might wish that we blushed a little less easily, or sweated a little less easily, or that we were a little less tense. These are the reactions which make us feel uncomfortable in some public situations. At the moment we have no control over them, and can do nothing about them. Would it be possible to take more control over these automatic reactions of our body?

Taking control

It is possible to be more in control of our reactions, and if you are shy, the benefits of gaining this control are immense. **If you are physically relaxed and at ease, you will also be mentally relaxed and at ease.** Wouldn't it be nice to be able to transmit an air of calmness and relaxation, to be able to put others at their ease simply by being comfortable with yourself? Wouldn't it be nice if someone were to say to you 'I wish I could be as relaxed as you are!' That would be worth working for.

You can achieve this goal. It isn't easy, but it can be done, and as before, if you can appear relaxed and at ease other people will assume that you are the urbane and sophisticated person that you seem to be. If you can play that role you will in time become less shy and more like the person you appear to be. This is not artifice or cheating, it is a natural progression in your task of overcoming shyness.

We are really back to discussing image, the sort of image you project in your encounters with other people. It doesn't matter who it is, whether it is a prospective boyfriend or girlfriend, or a client or your boss—if you seem to be in control of yourself, to be relaxed and at ease, you impress. Some shy people may actually be relaxed and at ease, but most are not. It doesn't matter whether you are tense or whether you are laid back, you can improve your performance, and learning to do that is an interesting and rewarding experience. How do you go about it? A young woman came to see me in my surgery one day. She was complaining of feeling tired all the time, and she wanted help.

Julie

Julie was a young woman who enjoyed life, or rather she had enjoyed life until she developed this terrible tiredness. She had put up with it for a long time, but eventually she had felt obliged to come to see her family doctor. Why was she so tired? It turned out that she wasn't suffering from any sort of physical illness, but even so there was a physical reason why she felt so tired. She felt tired because she *was* tired.

Now Julie wasn't doing anything different from what she usually did, but for some reason she had begun to experience this overwhelming feeling of tiredness. She went to bed feeling tired, she woke up feeling tired and she felt tired all day. It was a very unpleasant situation to be in, and it was hard for Julie to understand. Why on earth should she feel so tired? She was sleeping all night, but that didn't seem to make any difference. Julie's problem illustrates just how psychological factors can affect the way our bodies work, not just in the immediate situation as with sweating or blushing, but in the longer term.

I asked Julie to notice a few things about her physical state. I asked her to check the tension in her neck muscles in the morning by pressing them with her thumb. I asked her to check her cheek muscles in the same way, and to notice if her teeth were sore because she had been clenching her teeth all night, and I asked her to check whether she had nail marks on the palms of her hands from clenching her fists all night. It was no surprise to me at all when Julie came back and reported that all these things were happening. She was tense all night, and tense all day. She had been able to sustain this kind of tension for a long time, but eventually these physical sensations, such as tiredness, had surfaced and she had begun to feel ill.

Julie was a shy person, and she had personal problems related to her work. Over a period of time she had become stressed, and these background stresses, which were indirectly related to her shyness, had begun to cause problems. She had simply become physically tense, in all the muscles of her body, and she was now having difficulty coping. There is probably no reason why you should have that sort of tension, but it illustrates what can happen. It is a fair bet that you will be physically tense before a social event, or a date, or a meeting or something of that sort, and you might be like Julie and wake up in the morning on that particular day feeling unwell or uneasy, and just not know why. Check it out.

Physical sensations

If you are shy there is every possibility that you will feel uneasy in certain situations, situations in which your shyness causes you to be stressed. You will feel apprehensive, you will feel tense, you will have churnings in your tummy and you might have a tremor. You will recognize this collection of sensations as the sort of thing that you, or indeed anyone, would expect to experience before a stressful event, before you have to make a speech or a presentation, or before going on to the stage if you are an amateur actor or musician. You don't have to be shy to experience these sensations, but if you are shy you may experience them at times when other people might not, such as before an ordinary social event or a party.

Julie had these sensations all of the time, and they wore her down in the long term. Her body had learned to be tense all of the time. Although you might suffer from the same problem, the chances are that your body has only learned to be tense in certain specific situations—those which you find stressful, such as a party or a meeting. Now is the time to look more closely at the physical symptoms which you suffer as a result of your shyness.

Using your diary

As you might have guessed, before you can take any action to reduce these sensations and make yourself more comfortable in stressful situations, you have to find out exactly just what is happening, and that means keeping a diary. I would hope that you will by now have taken on the things we have been discussing and so will have the time to look at this new dimension to the problem of your shyness. Start making some notes. This is what Julie did as a start to overcoming her problem, and it is what you must do.

If you feel uncomfortable, either before an event or during an event, try to find out why. Think in purely physical terms. Are the muscles in your neck tense and sore? Is your tummy churning or do you have feelings of diarrhoea, or is it just that it's too hot so that you're sweating with that prickly feeling down your back? Make a note of what you actually feel, and in what situations you feel it. Keep a diary over a few weeks so that you have a good idea exactly what's going on. If you're going to be at your best for any event, you want to start by being in the best physical condition you can be in, and you want to be in control of your body. You want to gain that control for the short term, perhaps for the day of an event or maybe just for the duration of the event itself, or in the long term as in the case of Julie.

What are you likely to find out? One thing is just about certain: you will find that you experience an increase in muscle tension when you are stressed. Quite simply, you become tense. Your neck and shoulder muscles tighten up, and if you are tense enough you might even develop a tremor in your hands. This increase in tension occurs because your body produces too much of a substance called adrenalin, which is necessary in time of physical stress or danger when you have to react quickly and strongly, but which can be troublesome in times of psychological stress. Your body can't distinguish between the two conditions, so it assumes that when you are stressed you will either want to run away or to fight, and adrenalin is produced to increase your physical performance to equip you for both situations. It is less useful if you are sitting in a corner feeling shy and unhappy. What you really don't need in that situation is an increase in muscle tone, but unfortunately that is what you get, thanks to your adrenalin. Can you do anything about it?

Relaxing

It goes without saying that you should relax in these difficult situations, but how do you do that? You have no doubt tried to relax without having any success, and that isn't surprising because it's almost impossible to do unless you have learned how. Yet it would be very nice to be able to relax, and that should be the stimulus to actually take this problem on and do something about it. There is a way of tackling it, which takes time and effort, but it is worth a lot of both because overcoming this muscle tension is the key to being comfortable in stressful situations.

The problem is that when you are in such a stressful situation, it's too late to do anything about it. If you want to acquire the skill of relaxation, you have to start when you are in the quiet of your own home. When you have learned and practised the skill, you can then use it when you are in a stressful situation. You have to learn the art of relaxation, and incidentally of slowing and controlling your breathing, and you have to be prepared to put time and effort into your practice. There are no short cuts and there is no alternative, but think of the benefits. Think of being able to sit quietly and emanate an air of relaxed calm wherever you are. If you know that you can do that, along with the other skills you have learned, your confidence will soar and your shyness will melt like the winter snow in spring.

Relaxation exercises

If you can sleep all night and wake up tired because you have been clenching your fists and your jaw, it stands to reason that you can't relax during the day, particularly at stressful times, just by wanting to do so. There has to be some mechanism for achieving relaxation, and that's what you have to learn. Once you've learned that mechanism you can use it as a tool in difficult situations. You won't have to do all the exercises I am going to describe every time, but you have to start by learning the technique.

There are two advantages to learning relaxation techniques. The first is that you can learn to relax when you are tense. The second is that you can spot when you are becoming tense much earlier than you otherwise would and can thus relax before you become locked into tension. Relaxation techniques aren't the answer to all of your problems, but they can go a long way towards making you comfortable in stressful situations.

Do these exercises now. Read them through before you start, and then do them as you read them, making sure that they take about twenty minutes from beginning to end. If you can, dictate them into a cassette player at the speed you would do them, and relax to the sound of your own voice. Find a warm room and sit or lie down with your head supported. Make sure that you are warm and comfortable, slow your breathing, and begin the exercises.

The exercises

Start the exercises with your arms and hands. Start with your right hand by clenching your right fist. Hold it clenched for a moment and notice the sensations this produces, not only in your hand but in your lower arm. The palm of your hand, your knuckles and the back of your hand will feel tight, as will your lower arm. Hold that for a second and then suddenly relax your fist, letting your fingers hang down. Your hand and arm will now feel warm and heavy and relaxed. Keep your breathing slow and then slow it even more.

Now go to your left hand and repeat the exercise exactly as for the right hand, concentrating hard on the sensations produced by first clenching and then relaxing, and notice the heaviness and warmth in your hand after you have finished. Slow your breathing at the end of each section.

Now let's move on to your shoulders and neck. It is this area which is usually the first to become tense, and it is certainly the most uncomfortable. You will know how tense it can become by the pain you feel if you press your thumb into the muscles of your neck when you become uncomfortable at a public event, so pay particular attention to this area. Concentrate on your shoulders. Tighten them up and hold them in that uncomfortable raised position for a second or two, noticing the tension in your shoulders, neck and in the top part of your chest and back. Now, just as before, suddenly relax these muscles and let your arms and shoulders hang down. Notice the feeling of relaxation in your shoulders, back, chest and neck. Slow your breathing as before.

Now concentrate on your neck. Tense your neck muscles by pushing your head back until you can feel tension in the muscles in the front of your neck, but be careful not to push too hard. Again, relax your neck suddenly and notice the feeling of relaxation in the muscles. Move your head around so that it feels loose. Remember to slow your breathing.

Now tighten the muscles of your face. Frown and close your eyes as tightly as you can. Then increase the tension by clenching your teeth tightly, pressing your lips together and pressing your tongue into the roof of your mouth. Your whole face will feel tense, so when you suddenly relax these muscles you will notice how your forehead, cheeks, jaw and lips feel loose. Let your jaw sag slightly. Slow your breathing.

Now move on down your body. Arch your back slightly and pull in your tummy. Hold that tension for a few moments until you are aware of the feeling of tension in the muscles of your back and stomach. Now relax these muscles slowly and note what that feeling of relaxation is like in the muscles of your back and stomach. Take time to enjoy the sensation, and breathe more slowly.

Now we can move on down to the legs. Start with your right leg. Straighten it and push your foot and your toes away from you, and as before note the tension in your toes, your foot and your lower leg. Hold that tension and then relax it suddenly so that your foot and lower leg feels loose. Pause to enjoy the sensation before repeating the exercise with your left leg. Then slow your breathing.

Now you are getting to the end of your relaxation session, which should have taken about twenty minutes, and this is the time to concentrate on your breathing. Slow it down to about eight respirations per minute and note that your arms and legs are heavy. Your hands will feel warm and the muscles in your abdomen, back, neck and face will feel soft.

Think of a relaxing scene such as a warm beach or a warm room with a big comfortable armchair. Breathe in and out slowly, and as you breathe out think of the word 'calm'. Do that about 20 times. If you have achieved deep relaxation you will know because of the sensation of warmth in your hands and feet, and the overall sense of relaxation. When you are ready, finish the session gradually. Move your arms and legs and count down from 5 to 1, finishing by saying 'Wake up!' Your session is over.

Problems with relaxation

The most obvious problem with relaxation exercises is that they aren't easy to do and you may take some time before you can achieve adequate relaxation. If that is the case you just have to keep working at it. If you find that relaxation exercises make you go to sleep don't worry—if you can do that, the exercises must be working. Try to stay awake, but remember that you may be able to use these exercises to help you to get to sleep at night.

Another problem may be that when you get up and start to walk about, you get tense again. That often happens and it is difficult to sustain relaxation, but remember that you intend to use these techniques in difficult situations, so if you have learned relaxation techniques you have a tool which you can use when you are stressed. One way of improving your relaxation technique is to practise all the time. Do it in the car or on the train or at a meeting. You don't have to go through all the tensing and squeezing, you just have to mentally work round your body in the correct sequence, and if you have done your homework, and only if you have done your homework, you will be able to relax and to develop your relaxation skills.

If you find these exercises difficult you must keep at it. You have to develop the skill of relaxation if it is to be of use to you in real-life situations.

Using relaxation

No one could sit at a party doing all these tightening and clenching manoeuvres without appearing a little conspicuous. That isn't the idea at all, but once you have achieved physical control over the tension in your muscles you will be able to relax them at will, but remember that you have to practise—in the car, watching television or standing in a queue. Do it everywhere, and do it at the next social event you attend. Just let your shoulders come down, move your neck around, let your arms hang loose and let your legs go limp. Slow your breathing and think of the word 'calm'. Start to do that as soon as you begin to feel tense, or even before that.

Make a habit of always being calm. When you sit down in a chair think 'calm' and adjust your posture so that you are sitting comfortably. Relax, and try to radiate that relaxation to other people. Be relaxed, and look relaxed. People will know that you are relaxed, and you won't look shy. If you relax well, you won't feel shy, you will feel confident. You will now be in a position to use the other ideas we have discussed, to practise your conversational skills so that you are in control of the situation. Be relaxed. It isn't easy to learn the technique, but it's worth the effort. It is worth it because it is impossible to be physically relaxed and mentally tense, so that relaxation exercises relax the mind as well as the body.

There is another way by which you can become physically tense, and that is by overbreathing. That doesn't mean that you are panting, or gasping for air, it just means that when you are stressed, as a shy person may be at a party or social event, you may breathe a little more deeply than usual without being aware of it. In the process of overbreathing we expel more carbon dioxide than usual from our lungs and this alters your blood chemistry, producing a condition called tetany in which muscles become tense. That could make you uncomfortable in difficult situations. We have tried to control our breathing during the relaxation exercises for this reason as well as simply trying to contribute to the feeling of relaxation. There are separate breathing exercises we can use and it is worth learning them.

Breathing exercises

In a tense situation you may breathe faster than normal, breathe more deeply than normal, or you may have developed the habit of sighing frequently. You can learn to control your breathing. It takes effort but it can be done by practising breathing exercises.

For these exercises you don't need a private room. They are perhaps best practised whilst watching TV, but if you're watching with someone else you had better explain what you are doing! To learn these exercises, sit in a semi-reclining position, slouched and leaning back in a comfortable armchair. Relax.

When you are at rest you breathe with your tummy muscles, and although that seems strange, it is true. It is only when you are exercising that you use your chest muscles to raise and lower your ribs, forcing the air in and out of your lungs. If you are using these chest muscles in your semi-reclining position or at rest, then you are overbreathing.

In order to find out what is going on, place one hand on your chest, and the other one on your tummy. That's all you have to do. When you are in this position, notice which of your hands is moving. If it is your tummy hand you are breathing normally, but if it is your chest hand, you are overbreathing. Notice if you are taking frequent sighs.

Now all you have to do is to breathe slowly and quietly, trying to let your tummy hand do the moving. Try not to sigh or to breathe too rapidly. Just let yourself relax and breathe normally. Stay in this position as long as possible, because these skills aren't learned quickly. To change your breathing habits you first have to develop an awareness that you are overbreathing, and then do something about it, so that if you are at a party and you feel yourself getting tense, you can first use your relaxation techniques, and then if you seem to be overbreathing, you can check if you are using abdominal or chest muscles, and if necessary correct that.

These checks and techniques should become a matter of habit. You should hardly be aware that you are using them, but to reach that position you have to work and practise by yourself at home and at every other possible opportunity. Eventually you will become unaware that you are actively trying to relax or control your breathing and you will be naturally relaxed, and at that stage most of your problems will be over.

Other physical problems

Shy and tense people may have other physical problems related to the increased production of adrenalin by their bodies. They may blush easily, or sweat easily, and then there are more long-term problems like diarrhoea before a public event, or a hand tremor, or sometimes a feeling that they can't get a breath or that they can't swallow. These sensations are common in anxious people, and some shy people can on occasions be put under stress and feel anxious.

Learning relaxation techniques can be very helpful for most of these sensations, and for most of these unpleasant symptoms it may be all that can be done. It may be that your body has developed a habit of producing adrenalin too easily. Many of the body's functions are set by mechanisms which work like a thermostat on your central heating system, and if that 'thermostat' is made to be too sensitive, you produce adrenalin too easily so that it isn't only produced in situations of physical danger, it may also be produced at a party or even on the morning before a party. How do you reset it?

There is only one way of regaining control of your body, and that is by laboriously doing the relaxation exercises already described. If you work at it every day you can gradually reset that thermostat, and in time become comfortable again. Learning relaxation thus helps to control many of the other unpleasant feelings an anxious or a shy person may experience.

Seeking advice

If your shyness is really a problem, if it is ruining your life, you might consider seeking advice from an expert, but who can you consult? The most accessible professional is your own doctor, and he will be able to advise you himself or make arrangements for you to see someone else if he thinks they might be able to help. Such a person might be a psychologist, a professional with special knowledge of psychological problems. He or she will have special skills in treating all sorts of problems. You can of course consult anyone you choose, but remember that there are no short cuts, so that if anyone offers you a quick answer to your shyness, regard it with a degree of scepticism. Your problem didn't develop overnight, and it won't go away overnight.

If you have specific physical symptoms such as a tremor, which might be a problem for a musician for example, or if you have excessive diarrhoea in stressful situations, your doctor might be able to offer you medication which can be useful in the short term. There is however, no medical answer to blushing. If that is your problem, you have to manage it by relaxing, and by finding ploys for dealing with it. The best ploy is just to ignore it because it will be more obvious to you than to anyone else, and if you don't bring it to other people's attention they probably won't notice it. Other people are too concerned about their own problems, their piles or their fallen arches, to notice your difficulties.

And so....

An awareness that you are in control of your body, in control of the situation whatever it may be, and that you are projecting a relaxed urbane image simply by your presence, your ambience and the way you converse, means that you have come a long way from being the shy person you once were. Your confidence is growing, and it will continue to grow. The number of things that you may be prepared to attempt may have increased dramatically as your confidence has grown, and yet you still feel shy. That is something we must look at next.

REMEMBER:

- Every psychological condition has a physical component.
- It is possible to improve physical difficulties.
- Relaxing physically is a skill which can be learned.
- Being relaxed helps you to manage difficult situations.
- The more confident you are that you can manage social situations, the less shy you will feel.

Chapter 8

The psychological side of shyness

We have been considering shyness as being almost a physical condition, but that has been because we can deal with the physical side of shyness and make real progress quickly by doing so. That's all very well, but at the back of your mind has been the awareness that there is another aspect of shyness, something which is just as important, or even more important. It is also more elusive, more difficult to pin down, more difficult to deal with. Yet it is there. It is the psychological side of shyness, the mental awareness that you are shy.

If you have been taking the advice given in this book up to now, and if you have been doing the exercises, you will have been making progress and you will be more confident and more able than you were, and as a result you will be more comfortable in most situations and more in control. So far so good, but despite everything you may still feel shy and that can be disappointing. You really want to shake off this shyness, to rid yourself of that feeling forever, yet shyness adheres to your personality like glue. You seem to be stuck with it. Is there no way of getting rid of that feeling?

Give it time

The simple answer is that it takes time for the mental awareness of your shyness to go away, so you have to allow time, sometimes a long time, for that to happen. Your ability to go to meetings and social events, your competence, your desire to do these things, all will improve before you lose that feeling of shyness you get when you encounter a new situation. It has to be remembered also that no one has said they can change the core of your personality. Changing that would mean changing you into somebody else, and that isn't on the agenda. We are in the business of overcoming shyness, of defeating the affliction and of allowing your personality full expression, unfettered by the chains of excessive shyness. That will happen in time. In the meantime you will continue to work to overcome your shyness, but you will also have time to think about the nature of your shyness. It is an intriguing phenomenon.

The phenomenon of shyness

Shyness is very strange. It is possible to be aggressive and positive in many areas of life, but shy and diffident in others. One of the world's most famous film stars is also a recluse, known for his shyness. He rarely gives interviews, but in one interview that I saw he talked for a long time about the problems caused by being shy, and he was clearly being truthful. Yet this man is in constant demand because of his ability as an actor, one of the most public and exposed occupations imaginable. How can this be?

Many actors are shy, or claim to be. Many public performers are extremely nervous about appearing in public, and some may be physically sick before going on stage. It seems to be possible to compartmentalize shyness, to keep one part of one's self for public view whilst protecting one's real self behind a wall of shyness. That wall can only be penetrated by someone very close to you. There is something precious about our secret selves, and we don't expose that part of our personality easily. We feel vulnerable, we protect ourselves and this is true for everyone.

Defining shyness

We have tried to define shyness but somehow the definition eludes us, yet pinning something down by giving it a name and then describing it accurately is a fundamental first step in overcoming any problem. There are some things that we can say about shyness. Firstly, shyness can be very specific, and be related to some particular aspect of your relationships with other people, very often with members of the opposite sex. We are all familiar with the stereotype of the brilliant aspiring businessman or athlete who is reduced to a quivering wreck by the attentions of a woman, or of the female executive who is 'all fingers and thumbs' when a she meets a man in a social situation. Perhaps for such people shyness does run through all the aspects of their personality, but it is more manageable in some areas than in others, and if it is going to cause problems it will be in the difficult area of sex.

Shyness is also to do with lost confidence, or perhaps confidence that was never gained. Some people just don't feel that they are any good at some things, often a great number of things, and they give up trying. They have no confidence, and once confidence is lost it is hard to get it back. Then there is the fact that some people are better at doing certain things than other people, and that includes the social skills we have been talking about. For some people the small talk, the easy conversational gambit, the compliment all come easily; for others it just doesn't seem to work.

These skills which we need in our everyday exchanges have to be learned, and for some of us the opportunities to learn these skills were absent at a critical time. We may have led an isolated childhood because our parents didn't have an active social life, or because we lived somewhere where there were few other children to mix with. We may have learned to be timid from our parents so that we didn't begin to learn the social skills we needed until it was too late. There is an optimum time for learning anything, and if you miss that time, it is hard to catch up. We have talked a lot about learning, both as a method of overcoming our shyness, and as a mechanism for the way our shyness is produced in the first place. That is entirely logical. If shyness has been learned, or at least in part learned, then it can be unlearned.

Shyness in certain situations

Clues as to the nature of shyness can be found in the fact that it works in some situations more than in others. It is specific in its action. We have considered sexual encounters as a source of shy behaviour. Shyness is often associated with sex. The nature of sexual attraction, of the awareness of one's own sexuality and the sexuality of others, is mysterious indeed. Watch the reactions of a group of men if an attractive woman enters the room. They will all be aware of her presence, and in small ways they will all react. Even the most macho of those present may appear shy, almost as if he is dazzled by her arrival. Sexual awareness and attractiveness are powerful and ever-present phenomena, and they can be very difficult to deal with for members of both sexes. It isn't surprising that some of us don't quite get it right.

If an attractive member of the opposite sex, or even any member of the opposite sex, can give some of us problems with our shyness, so can aggressive behaviour in others. An aggressive boss, an aggressive man in a bar, a shop assistant or even a double glazing salesman on the other end of a telephone—they can all intimidate us and make us aware of our shyness. The prospect of having to deal with such people makes us feel shy. Aggression is something which shy people often can't handle in a reasoned or sensible way, and it is something they often don't handle to their own satisfaction.

Another problem is that of having to put one's self forward, to have to give a public performance of any sort, be it a stage performance or having to make a speech or, even worse, being on the receiving end of an award or commendation. Shy people are private people, and they are unwilling or unable to expose themselves. They can use acting, or some similar activity, to disguise their true selves by pretending to be someone else, as our Hollywood actor may have done. Many great actors seem to be able to act out their emotions on the stage or on camera rather than in life, and some only really live when they are 'in character'. We cannot all be actors, but there are occasions when we have to perform in public as ourselves, and that can be painful for a shy person.

The real nature of shyness

Is there a 'bottom line' to all these aspects of shyness? If we can understand it, will it help us to change our mental attitude to our shyness so that we can live fuller and happier lives, and also get rid of that underlying mental awareness of our shyness? If there is such a thing as the essential nature of shyness, it must take the form of a profound unwillingness to expose our inner selves. We hold on tightly to our emotions, which is why sexual encounters can be so difficult. We have to keep control because we don't want anyone to see through to the deepest and most vulnerable core of our personality. Shy people are vulnerable and easily hurt. They care very much about what others think of them, and they do not want to hurt other people's feelings by saying or doing something which would produce that effect. Clearly, these are not unattractive attributes. The world needs shy people.

The problem lies in the balance of these features in our personality. If our shyness leads on to feelings of inferiority, or to a poor self-image, or if it reduces our performance or holds us back at our work, or if most of all it stops us from making friends or having normal sexual relationships, then we have to look at our attitudes and at our self-image as well as at the practicality of our shyness, which is what we have been concentrating on up to now. Let's look at three people whose shyness became a problem they felt they had to solve.

Raymond

Raymond was nineteen years of age. He was energetic, played rugby and cricket and would have excelled at any other sport, was academically bright and was considered by most to be a potential leader. No one would have thought that Raymond had any problems, but he knew that he had, and that is why he came to talk to me.

His problem of course was that he was shy. No one would have guessed that he was shy, and to many the thought would have been inconceivable. He was just too successful, but his real success was in disguising the fact of his shyness from everyone, even his closest friends. He had mastered the art of presenting a positive image, and he was able to give a competent performance, but within himself he had the mental awareness of his shyness. He had little confidence, particularly when it came to personal matters. The grand public performance was no problem because he was a good actor, and he was naturally good at sport so that was no problem. At a party he could dominate by the strength of his personality and by his reputation, and he could even bluff his way with girls, but there was a limit. Deep down he felt vulnerable, and there was part of himself which he kept to himself.

The fact is that nobody got to know him very well. People thought they knew him and he had many acquaintances, but he really had no close friends, something which surprised people when it was pointed out to them. It was, however, something of which Raymond was acutely aware. As he got older, he became more bothered by his inability to make friends, and in particular girlfriends. He could take a girl out on a date, but he could never be intimate with a girl and he got a reputation for being fickle with women. In a way it enhanced his image, and to those who noticed he became something of an enigma.

Raymond was intelligent, and he knew exactly what was going on. In that respect he was lucky because many people never get this sort of insight, but Raymond knew that he was shy, and he knew that he would have to do something about it because he was getting into deeper and deeper trouble. He was beginning to avoid some situations which he found particularly difficult, and as everyone else seemed to be pairing off and forming relationships, Raymond, with all his ability and all his insight, was becoming more and more isolated.

Jennifer

Jennifer was a girl of sixteen. She was a quiet girl, and everyone who knew her said that she was shy. She was withdrawn, reticent and she tended to stay at home when others were out at parties or at the cinema. It wasn't that she wanted to be a recluse, it was just that she found social encounters difficult and so she tended to avoid them. If she had been asked she wouldn't have been able to explain why she didn't go out as much as her friends, and indeed she probably wouldn't have agreed that was the case. When she didn't go out she always had a good reason: because she had a cold, or she had something important to do. She had no boyfriends, and rarely had any contact with boys.

Jennifer was an attractive girl, she was bright and able, and in her own way she was popular and well-liked, but people had noticed that she was becoming more and more withdrawn. Eventually her friends stopped asking her out, and she was left to her own devices. At first this suited her very well. The pressure of having to go out and mix socially with others was removed, and she could stay quietly in the safety of her own home. It wasn't very long however before this lifestyle began to pall. She knew that life was passing her by, and she became jealous of her friends and the enjoyment they seemed to be getting out of life. She became morose and irritable. She snapped at people, and at last even her friends stopped trying to help her.

She realised that she would have to do something, that life just wasn't satisfactory and she could see disaster looming, and fortunately she had the sense to seek help. She had major problems, but they weren't insoluble, and as she had the desire and the will to set about solving them, the prospects for a dramatic improvement were very good.

Simon

Simon was older than the two other people we have considered. He was in his mid-thirties, married and held a good position in a prestigious company. He was well-respected, but he had the reputation of being a formal, rather stiff individual. He wore dark suits, not only to work but also at the weekends, and would never have turned up at any sort of public event in anything but what he considered to be proper dress—his suit. His wife, by contrast, was well-liked and outgoing, and was heavily involved in many local events. It was widely thought that Simon's wife was good for him, and that she helped him to be more human and relaxed than he might otherwise be.

Life was good to Simon. He was obviously good at his job, he had a very satisfactory income and a house and car to match. He had two children, both boys, and the family seemed to be healthy and happy. Then Simon was made redundant. His world collapsed; people wondered what would happen. Initially not much did happen. The terms of Simon's redundancy were generous, so there were no immediate financial worries. He continued as if nothing had happened, wore the same clothes, continued with the same interests he had before. He spoke freely about his misfortune, and people were sympathetic. His friends thought that he had managed the disaster very well, and assumed that with his talents and experience he would soon get another job. As time went on he didn't manage to find alternative employment, and eventually he came to talk to me about his problems.

There were no surprises about Simon's difficulties. He had some insight into his problem, and what it really boiled down to was the fact that he was now, and always had been, immensely shy. He had been able to deal with his shyness by assuming this very formal persona, but when he was stressed, and even with the excellent and enlightened support of his wife, he again became shy to the extent that he couldn't manage social contacts, and even worse, he couldn't manage interviews. He was becoming more reclusive and less likely to get a job. He really needed help.

What has gone wrong?

What do you think has been the problem for these three people? In some respects they share the same problem, and it should be fairly obvious just what that problem was. In some ways, it is easier to see what has gone right than what has gone wrong. Raymond was the sort of person just about every boy would like to be. He was popular and successful, admired by everyone, and if he was shy he had already done just about everything recommended in this book to begin to overcome the problem. He had an outgoing positive image, he had all the social skills and in many respects he was very confident.

Jennifer was more obviously shy. She avoided social contacts and lived an increasingly isolated existence. She, like Raymond, had developed a lifestyle which was satisfactory in the first instance, but in time it became more unsatisfactory and she eventually was unable to sustain it. In that respect she had the same problem as Raymond.

Simon had likewise been forced to abandon a lifestyle which had been satisfactory, though in his case this had been for external reasons. He had developed a precarious way of dealing with a common problem, and the same is true of both Jennifer and Raymond. They had done almost everything right, but they had missed one essential point, the key to overcoming their shyness. They had made a fundamental mistake, and one which you should be careful to avoid. They had used their considerable abilities to present themselves in the most positive way they could, and that was even true of Jennifer. They had used their ability to cover up their shyness, to avoid facing up to it, and the kernel of that shyness remained in the depths of their personality.

The psychological side of shyness

The three people we have discussed managed to hide their vulnerability behind a false image. It was a satisfactory image as far as they were concerned, and it offered them short-term gains, but in the long run it wasn't possible for them to sustain it. They had used their abilities to build a wall around their shyness, a wall which excluded the very people they wanted to admit. For Raymond, he had been so successful in building his image that he simply couldn't let anyone see that he was less than perfect. Jennifer was quite happy to be thought of as a recluse and wouldn't consider letting that image slip, and Simon was the terribly efficient and reliable executive and member of the community. His entire reputation depended on his always being right, always reliable and always efficient. Could they have done things differently?

It is impossible to overstate the importance of honesty—honesty with oneself that is—in the construction of a public persona. We haven't much say in these things under normal circumstances, that image just develops, and it is quite possible that our three didn't choose to present the image they did—it simply emerged to satisfy the requirements of their personality. It wasn't a totally honest image though. Raymond wasn't happy as the perfect man, Jennifer wasn't happy as the recluse, and Simon wasn't happy as the totally efficient businessman. They could manage but the psychological side of their shyness was still lurking in the background to annoy them. It would have been much better if they could have in some way admitted to themselves, and to others, that they were vulnerable, and that they needed comfort and help from other people. Everyone depends on others, and as they say, no man is an island—and no woman either.

I have suggested that you actively create an image and hone your social skills to create a public persona which will allow you to appear less shy and so feel more confident. You run the risk of being so successful that you may be able to use that persona to protect your vulnerability. That isn't the idea at all. You have to take your shyness along with you, to recognize it and allow that it is part of you. You have to be able to confess it, to ask for advice or help, to be flexible and to be prepared to learn.

It takes a lot of confidence to admit that you have problems, particularly if you are young, so use the confidence-building exercises to help you to bring out your shyness. You don't want to flaunt it, but you have to be prepared to recognize it and allow selected people, perhaps a girlfriend or a boyfriend, to know who you really are. You have to let the barriers down sometime, to be human and vulnerable. You have to be able to take that risk. The three people we mentioned earlier weren't. They simply ignored the psychological side of their shyness.

Living a lie

It is possible to take this false image further and live a life which is a complete lie. There are people who decide for one reason or another that they should be intellectual, or that they should be the outdoor type, or that they should be sporting when in fact their inclination is to be precisely the opposite. They may have followed friends down the path to an inappropriate lifestyle, seeing how successful these friends have been and wishing to emulate that success, or they may at some critical time in their lives have wanted to impress someone, a parent or a girlfriend or boyfriend, and then become caught up in a whole way of life which is simply wrong for them. They are trapped in a phoney way of living often by chance, and they aren't aware of what has happened.

Such people may or may not be shy, but if they are shy there is every possibility that they are using their adopted lifestyle to conceal their shyness even from themselves. They fall into the same category as those people who are deliberately concealing their shyness from themselves and from everyone else, and simply not facing up to the psychological reality of their shyness. They, like everyone else, have to come down to earth, have to enter the real world where people meet people in an honest and straightforward way, the only way in which true relationships can be formed. If they can do that they are lucky. In the words of the popular song:

'People who need people,
Are the luckiest people in the world.' It's true!

Finding yourself

Most individuals fall into these traps by accident, though if you are trying to project a more positive image it is something you might do deliberately or in error. In all things you have to be yourself, but then who is your real self? How do you know who you are? It sounds as if it would be impossible to work that out without coming to a completely subjective conclusion, but is that really the case? Is it impossible to make an objective assessment of yourself? I think that most of us have a fair idea of what we are really like. We can hide it from ourselves, but if we sit down and try to see ourselves as others see us, we can get close to an understanding of what we are like. We have to make an intellectual assessment, we have to cut away the things we have added to our personality for our convenience, and see what we are like in real life.

We can get help by comparing ourselves to others, seeing how we measure up. We can use our imagination to conjure up the sort of lifestyle which would be more appropriate, and we can do it honestly. If we set out to do just that, doing it deliberately, maybe during a relaxation session, then yes, we can achieve it.

Who do you think you are?

Finding yourself can be a very difficult and traumatic experience. We all have some illusions about ourselves and it would be a cruel world if we were only allowed the truth. As you get older you become more accepting of the truth and it somehow doesn't seem so important that we conform, or that we put up a front. If you are shy it is in your own best interests to be honest with yourself and try to avoid having to live up to ideals which are inappropriate for you. It is equally important that you don't underestimate yourself and assume that you are less able than you really are. You must not undersell yourself. How can you get an objective view of yourself and decide on an image of yourself with which you can be comfortable and which you can sustain?

One way is to discuss it with friends, but that isn't easy. You may not have any close friends, or your friends may not be sympathetic to this sort of introspective rumination. If you are in business and seeking employment you can pay professionals a small fortune to analyse your personality and advise you of your strengths and weaknesses, but not many people can afford to do that, or would trust a stranger, no matter how expert, to make those judgements.

If you don't have the benefit of advice from friends, you have to rely upon your own initiative, but if you are going to assess your own personality and your own potential, you have to have some system for doing it. As with so many things, that means writing something down and working through the problem with the aid of pencil and paper.

You could of course make out a questionnaire and interrogate yourself, but that's a little harsh. A more satisfactory way is simply to write a few paragraphs about yourself and the things that you do under different headings, such as sport, leisure, work, holidays, reading, friends, girlfriends or boyfriends, and whatever else you think might be relevant. Write enough to give you an overall impression of the sort of life you are leading. Go into some detail so that you have a few pages to consider. At the end you will have a short essay about a very interesting subject—yourself. At the end read it through and make a few comments about the sort of person who lives this life.

When you are feeling strong, mark it like an essay. Start at the beginning and work through it, making comments upon whether or not the things you have mentioned are really things that you enjoy, whether you meet people when you are pursuing them, whether they represent a satisfactory use of your time and whether it is worth your while continuing with them. At the end, make a note about whether the lifestyle you first described is the most suitable for the person you are, and in the light of your comments try to write a few words about the person you really are, which might be slightly different from your notes about the person who is living your life. Are you and the person who you first described one and the same, or are you living a lie?

The logical conclusion to this exercise is to do the reverse of what you have just done and write a few paragraphs about the sort of person you are, and then write about the sort of interests you should be pursuing based on the introspective research you have just been doing. You may not have spent much time in the past thinking about yourself in a constructive way, and although it's not something I would recommend that you spend too much time on, getting yourself and your life into some sort of perspective is of value. Looking at your life helps you to get to know yourself.

It is very easy to drift into a lifestyle which just isn't appropriate. It may satisfy your friends, it may even satisfy you and allow you to avoid situations you find difficult, but is it the best you can do for yourself, particularly when you are trying to deal with your shyness? No one leads an ideal life. We all do things out of a sense of duty, or because our friends do them, or just because they are available. Perhaps you should be doing the things that you really want to do.

Changing

When we know who we are, when we know how shy we are, only then can we think about changing ourselves. That doesn't mean contriving a false new personality, it means cutting away some of the pretence from our present personality and letting a little honesty shine through. It would be nice if we could be relaxed and lead the sort of life we really need. If we could do that friendships would just happen, relationships would form out of mutual interests, and we would be much more comfortable. We can't dramatically change our lives, but we can be open to the possibility of change so that when the opportunity arises we can take it, and in time improve our lives by natural evolution.

REMEMBER:

- There is a mental component to shyness which may remain after you have solved the physical problems.
- Don't live a lie—don't be embarrassed to admit to your shyness in the right circumstances.
- Be honest with yourself and with people close to you.
- Be open to the possibility of changing your life.

Chapter 9

Expanding your horizons

We have come a long way down the road towards the point where we can say that we have finally overcome our shyness, but we still have part of that journey to make. We have put in a great deal of effort in very practical ways; what you need now are some practical results. There has to be some reward for all that effort, and you should have now reached a stage where you can claim that reward.

If you are to take full advantage of the efforts you have made you have to add another ingredient. That ingredient is courage, but please don't misunderstand—I know that shy people exercise great courage in their everyday lives. It isn't easy being shy, and just managing from day to day makes demands on a shy person that someone who isn't shy could only guess at. Being shy is painful. What is required now is a different kind of courage, the courage to let go.

In the last chapter we saw how shy people can continue to protect that vulnerable centre of their persona against all odds, constructing a whole personality and lifestyle in order to do so. They really desperately want to keep part of themselves private. That is quite acceptable. Everyone has some part of themselves which is private, even from a boyfriend or girlfriend, even from a wife or husband. Nobody gives up everything, but shy people feel the need to hold on to too much. They find any contact which is too personal very threatening and they back off, put up the shutters and retreat into their shyness. That is something we have to rectify.

Building on achievements

If you have been working on the exercises in this book you will have equipped yourself with the tools to overcome this most basic of problems. You may have been working hard, and you may have been having great success, but at the end of the day you might also have come up against a brick wall. You may have failed to break through into a world where your shyness has ceased to be a problem. That last and most important step is the one which takes most courage.

You have achieved a lot. You have insight into your shyness. You have knowledge. You know that progress is possible because you have proved it for yourself and that is the only kind of proof which is acceptable. You owe it to yourself to keep up the momentum and make the most important push which will finally relieve you of the burden of shyness. As always, there is nothing spectacular to be done, nothing amazing, just the continuation of things we have talked about before, building on our past achievements.

Being well-equipped

If you are to make further progress you have to be prepared to hazard yourself, and if you are to do that you have to be well-prepared. You need a little confidence, you need to know that you can successfully do the things that you want to do and intend to do. That means being physically prepared—you already know how to relax, you have worked on your skills and can manage disasters, and it means being mentally prepared. You also have to be a the right frame of mind. So far we have avoided platitudes like 'Think Positively'. You can't control what you think about or how you think, but if you have been making progress along the lines we have been suggesting, your attitudes will have changed of their own accord. You will want to build on your achievements, you will want to do more and, most of all, you will want to reap some kind of reward for your efforts. A lot of the work in changing your attitudes will have been done without you knowing it. How do you capitalize on your success? How do you capitalize on the skills you have laboured so hard to acquire?

Moving on

It is an unfortunate fact that your ability to do things, to handle difficult situations and cope with disasters, comes good before the psychological awareness of your shyness disappears, so getting rid of that sensation of shyness is the last and the most difficult part of your programme. It is difficult to get rid of, and you can't just wish it away. You may have been protecting it without being aware of it, but a simple awareness that this is happening may be enough to raise the phenomenon into your consciousness and make you want to solve the problem. The question is: how?

There are no psychological tricks which will do the job for you. As in most other things, it is hard labour which triumphs in the end. You can help yourself by trying to be more open, by admitting to yourself and then to other people close to you that your shyness is a problem. Again you have to be careful to whom you admit such personal details about yourself, and you should be careful not to frighten off new friends by being too candid. Other people do like to help, do like to encourage a friend. It makes them feel good, so give people the opportunity to help you.

Group identity

If you have been able to get out and about and gain in confidence by doing some of the exercises in this book, you may well have been making a few new friends or acquaintances, and this may well be the most positive thing that you have done or could do, particularly if you are young. Young people operate best in groups, and there is a reason for that.

A group of people develops an identity of its own. This can be demonstrated very easily at educational or training events where there is almost always an obligatory session of group work, and it is the central fact which makes group therapy so useful in the treatment of some psychological states. A group of people, either in a formal setting or even in such a situation as on a holiday, develops a personality and a character all of its own. The individual members of the group make their personality subservient to that of the group, and the group will give support to its individual members.

In many organizations groups are very important. If the group is small enough, maybe a sales team or a platoon in the army, then an *esprit de corps* develops which makes the members of the group perform more effectively than they would do in isolation. Shy people tend to become rather isolated. If they become members of a group they tend to hang back and not take advantage of the benefits that membership of the group bestows. The group may make progress, but the shy person may remain an outsider. How does a group work?

The members of a group will automatically interact, and if they are given a task they will attempt to solve it by discussion in the first instance. Certain individuals in the group will initially make all the running, but in time the group will assert its authority and if someone is attempting to dominate it that person may become isolated. Often it is a more moderate and perhaps more reticent person who will eventually articulate the views of the group, and he or she will become the leader. The group will then consolidate behind that person, and each member will feel safe enough to contribute his or her opinions, so that the views of the group will evolve and develop. Each individual becomes recognized as being able to make a particular contribution, and his or her opinion will be sought by the group when it is appropriate. In that way every member of the group is seen to have a value, and each member can gain strength from the mutual trust and respect which the group bestows on its members.

If you are a member of such a group you can watch this process in action, and you will be expected to participate in it. It is a very good place to use the social skills you have been learning because a group, once it has become established, is very safe. If you aren't a member of such a group, either at work or in a club, it might be worth joining one, particularly if you have an interest such as photography or drama. A group is a good place for a shy person, particularly if that person is prepared to participate in and to use the group. We will consider groups again later.

Doing more

If you are to benefit from the progress you have already made, you will have to change your life. You will have to expand your activities, you will have to do more. Like just about everything else, that isn't as easy as it sounds, and that's why it takes courage. If you are normally reticent with few social outlets, you will have to find some, and you will have to find the right ones. That may take a little trial and error, but in the long run your happiness depends upon you finding new social outlets and developing a new social life.

Getting a more ambitious social life off the ground is as full of pitfalls and difficulties as anything else. There is the potential for mistakes and embarrassment, but then you have been training for just this. You have social skills, confidence and disaster limitation plans. You are able to make conversation, probably better than most people because you have been practising. If you are going into a new situation you will have done some homework and you will know who may be there and what the conversation is likely to be about. Don't forget about all that we have discussed in previous chapters—this is the time when all the practice by yourself, all the time spent learning relaxation and breathing, has now to be used. You have to expand your horizons.

Getting organized

Many of the things we do in this life are a matter of habit. We all develop habits of dress, of speech and in the things that we do. We also tend to avoid things which we find unpleasant, quite understandably. Breaking bad habits is a difficult task. We have already made an impact on some of our habits, but we must now deal with what is perhaps the most difficult, the habits we have in the organization of our social life. We have to develop and expand the things that we do, even if we do that as an exercise to help us to overcome our shyness. We have to break the chains of shyness, and if we are to do that we have to get out and about, we have to live a bit and if we do that we will feel more liberated, our confidence will grow, and our shyness will disappear.

So how do we get started? We want to get some degree of organization into our lives, so we must look around for ways to expand our activities. The sort of activity we might choose depends upon the individual, but there are some rules. If you want to expand your activities, don't choose something at random. You have to choose some occupation in which you have an interest. The old cliché is: 'Why don't you take up photography?' That's fine if you have a lasting interest in photography, but not everyone has. You might be interested in sport, or in cars or in horses or in anything. Everyone in this world has some interest. It might be in travel and holidays, or in drinking in the local pub; there are all sorts of things in which we might have an interest. There is no point in having a private hobby: you have to get amongst other people. A shy person, like an alcoholic, always has the threat of his affliction hanging over him and he, or she, cannot afford the luxury of a life of isolation. Start looking around.

Choosing

The idea is not to test yourself, not to test your new skills or your new confidence, so choose something non-threatening to start with. It shouldn't be too difficult. There is probably something which you always intended to join. You may be at a university or college and have a huge range of activities to choose from, or you may live in an isolated place where there are few opportunities to do the sort of thing you might want to do. What you should *not* do is radically change your lifestyle. Don't suddenly leave home or change your job. That might be the best thing for you to do in the long term, but for now, make haste slowly.

Even if there are no ideas which come readily to mind you should try to expand your activities. There will be things you haven't thought of such as becoming a youth group leader, or taking up a sport. Let the ideas emerge, but if you are younger and want to seek the company of members of the opposite sex, bear that in mind when you make your choice. If you have severe problems with your shyness it might be easier for you to be in the company of older people, because they are less threatening.

There are other things to think about, things like holidays and travel. The world is full of things to do and interests to foster, and you should not be intimidated by them. You should decide what things you might be doing if it weren't for your shyness, and then what things you might reasonably expect to do now that you have taken on your shyness, and lastly what things might help you to overcome your shyness. If you still have trouble finding one or two activities which you might pursue, what can you do? The answer should be obvious—you make a list.

Writing things down concentrates the mind. Make a short-term interim list of things that you might want to do, things that are available. Now score them, points for and points against. Try to think of all options, however unlikely, such as a political party. Organizations such as that have a strong sense of camaraderie and they are delighted to have new members. The same is true for most clubs or societies. New members are made most welcome, sometimes embarrassingly so, though this can be a problem in itself for a shy person. The important thing is to choose something, to make a move, and to get going. What happens next?

What can you expect?

The painful truth is that some aspects of your shyness will remain. No matter how much you prepare, and of course you should prepare, when it comes to the real situation there will be some apprehension, and when you are at a meeting or a party or a dance, you may still have some mental or even physical awareness of your shyness. It takes a long time for that to go, and you can't afford to wait forever. That's why you need courage. You have to grit your teeth and say to yourself that you are going to go out and then really do it, even if you are apprehensive and your stomach is churning. You have to say to yourself that you do have the skills, and that you do have the confidence, and that you can do it. And of course you can.

The feelings of apprehension and discomfort don't last, and once you are at an event, if you follow the routine you have practised, you will quickly begin to feel at home. If you have come to the right place you will be at home, and you will be made welcome. If you are very lucky you may meet somebody with whom you empathize, and you are off and running. Those feelings of shyness slide away and you can come off autopilot and fly by yourself, playing it by ear. You play yourself in and when you are comfortable you can take risks, be bold, manage the conversation in any way you want. But what opportunities are available for a shy person to branch out and find a fuller life?

Branching out

You may have used pencil and paper to make lists of all the possible areas for expanding your life. Even so, such a list can be daunting and it can be difficult to choose, and even when you do choose it can be difficult to decide how to manage a new situation. It is disappointing and disconcerting if you get it wrong on the first attempt, though by no means a disaster. Branching out can mean different things for different people. Raymond, the boy in the last chapter, was proficient in almost everything and could handle any situation except one, and that was forming a relationship with a girl. His starting point was very high on the scale of achievement, but even he had some new ground to cover. He had to find situations where he could develop the art of being intimate, and that was a big step for him.

It may be that you begin a little lower down the scale, and that you have different problems. For everyone the problems are different and the solutions different, but there are some general rules, or rather some advice which might help most people. Let's look at some common situations which most people, keen to try new experiences, might encounter.

Holidays

Holidays are important. We need holidays: they give us a break from our daily toil and they offer excitement and the possibility of romance. There are all sorts of holidays, so many that at first it might seem impossible to choose. Holidays give everyone, including shy people, a chance to be somebody else, to go where no one knows them, to do things they just wouldn't do at home. For a shy person there are traps. Holidays can be very testing, and the idea that a holiday is relaxing is not necessarily true. How can you get it right?

It's easier if you go on holiday with a friend. At least you won't have to bother about the problem of being lonely. Whether you have anyone to go on holiday with or not, you will have to choose very carefully. There are endless holidays advertised which seem to be for young people seeking friends, and they may well be excellent holidays for some people. I suspect that they are not for the very shy. The enforced jollity and camaraderie, the implied possibility of sexual liaisons, all these things might put unacceptable pressure on a shy person. These holidays are one long party, and if you aren't too keen on parties it would be best to avoid them. So what can you do?

The best idea might be a holiday where you have something to do. The most popular of this type is the skiing holiday where you have something to do all day, and at night there is the après-ski. If you are a beginner you are still part of a group, and you will develop a group identity so friendship will come naturally. If you are athletic, you might consider that option, or you might consider a watersports holiday in the summer if you prefer a holiday in the sun. There are all sorts of activity holidays in different countries. Holidays of the 'trekking' type inevitably mean a group of people incarcerated in a lorry, and as with any group you may be lucky in your companions, and you may not be. If you go on this type of holiday you will need all your social skills, but it might be a magnificent experience, something to remember for the rest of your life. Holidays closer to home offer the opportunity of more lasting friendships, though in general holiday romances don't last. Like the wine you enjoy so much in the foreign resort, they don't always travel.

The important thing is to decide to go on holiday. If shyness has been holding you back, simply do it. Decide to go, then decide who you are going to go with and where you are going to go. Don't let shyness stand in your way.

There's more to holidays than just the time they occupy. There is the anticipation, and there are the memories. If you are going to ski, there are the weeks of winter ski classes or time on the dry ski slopes and the possibility of a new hobby and a new interest. Use your holiday to push back the frontiers of your shyness.

Sport

It's never too late to take up a new sport. In this day and age there is a sport for everyone, and there are many advantages to taking up a physical activity. If you are fit you feel good. If you are successful you feel good. If you are a member of a team you make friends and that is good. If you have never considered taking up a sport, it is something you might consider. Even if it's just your local aerobics class you will get fit and you will meet new people, and if you are shy about your body sport might make you feel happier with it.

Shy people are a little more reticent than most about taking their clothes off and joining in this sort of activity. After all, clothes offer protection and provide an identity whilst a leotard does the opposite. All the more reason for buying a leotard. If you are slightly coy or embarrassed about your body, and some people are, swimming is a possible alternative.

The sheer physical enjoyment of exerting yourself, of making yourself physically tired instead of mentally exhausted is worth working for, and if you are less embarrassed at the end of the day that is an added advantage.

You have to use your sport to help with your shyness. You can go along to an aerobics class and stay entirely by yourself, but that is self-defeating. You have to go with the intention of making friends even if that means introducing yourself to the people around you.

You and your body

If you are shy about your body, that is something you should work on, and you can do that in the same way you tackle the other problems of shyness. Your body is meant to be enjoyed, and it is certainly nothing to be ashamed of, no matter what shape it might be. As you get older you become less sensitive about your body, but a young person can be very sensitive about their physique and embarrassed about exposing their anatomy to public view. It's as if no one else had a body, had breasts or genital organs. Obviously everyone has the same physical shape, and people will be less interested in yours than you think.

If you feel embarrassed about your body, take your clothes off. It might be more convenient to do this in the privacy of your own home, and it might avoid the possibility of getting arrested! Look at yourself in that mirror. It's time you learned to be a bit of a poser. Do you see anything to be ashamed of or embarrassed about? If you do, the embarrassment is in your eyes only. Shyness about the human body is very subjective. If you were a doctor or a nurse you would soon come to see the human body as a machine needing treatment with no other overtones at all, yet in a personal situation a body can be quite different.

You have to sort these little problems out. Your body will be fine on a Mediterranean beach, or in a leotard at the aerobics class, or at the swimming pool, or in a tight dress. You know that there will be times when your body will be an object of sexual attraction both for men and women, depending entirely on the situation and what you want it to be. Decide to make a feature of your body if you do feel that way inclined, taking up weight training or getting a tan, things which you can do privately. Eventually you will have to do more, so buy that exotic leotard, the teeny bikini, swimming trunks or shorts, know that you can look relaxed, and don't be shy.

More about sport

Another way of enjoying sport is to join a club. Clubs have an identity and a way of involving new members in their activities. If you go rock-climbing, for example, you will find a strong group identity because members of a rock-climbing group are physically dependent upon each other, and strong friendships can result. Team games are similar in that a team has an identity and an *esprit de corps* which can be useful to a shy person.

If you are going to take up a sport, either to get fit or, better still, to get fit *and* to help to overcome your shyness, choose something in which you are interested and which you really want to do. It would be self-defeating to try to take up any hobby in which you didn't have an interest. If you aren't interested in sport, why not try something else?

Clubs

Shy people aren't gregarious, but it might be better for them if they made the effort and joined some kind of social or special interest group. Societies can be difficult. Sometimes they aren't what they seem because the people involved in them aren't what you might expect, and you may not have as much in common with them as you expected.

Nonetheless, if you want to make a start, joining a club or society might be a good idea. If you have a special interest, then it certainly would be a good idea. If you want to develop a skill, you need the advice and support of a group.

One of the most useful new skills you can develop must certainly be public speaking.

Public speaking

Public speaking doesn't just mean making speeches, it means speaking in public in all sorts of situations from a business meeting or lecture to a wedding reception or even a grand speech at the opening of a factory or some great public occasion. It doesn't matter what it is; for the shy person or the nervous person, it can be a nightmare. It can make a shy person feel physically ill for days before the event, and it can cause the most disastrous of physical symptoms at the time of the speech. It can turn a simple departmental meeting at work into an ordeal. If you are going to expand your activities, you should really learn how to deal with this problem.

Learning to manage public speaking can be one of the most difficult challenges you will meet. Why should public speaking be so terrifying? I don't know the answer to that question, but it is difficult for everyone, even the most seasoned public speaker, and don't let anyone tell you otherwise. I imagine that it's difficult because someone speaking in public is so exposed. When you stand up to speak the room goes quiet, every eye turns towards the speaker, everyone is listening and the speaker is absolutely on his or her own. The speaker has to perform, and if he gets it wrong, it is a very public disaster.

A speech can go wrong for anyone, and we have all suffered the embarrassment of having to listen to a speech which didn't work. It isn't a situation we would wish to get into, yet there is always a risk to public speaking. There is always the chance that you might 'die', and even making a few remarks from the back of the hall at a public meeting can be difficult, with the chance that you might dry up, stutter, gag, or simply forget what you stood up to say. We are in the business of preparation, presentation and damage limitation.

Let's deal first with the formal speech, something that is planned weeks or months in advance. Formal occasions are bad for shy people because there tends to be no escape route and because people involved in the event are conspicuous. Speaking at a formal event can be tough. How can you minimize the difficulties? Begin by understanding that there *are* difficulties, and that that is true for everyone, no matter how experienced. Public speaking is stressful: the speaker will produce adrenalin, his hand will shake and he will sweat. Before the event he will have feelings of diarrhoea. That is the real situation, and we have to live with that reality and deal with it, but then we are experienced campaigners and this is one area where we can have an advantage over other people who have no experience in dealing with this sort of problem.

The elements needed to deal with this problem are good preparation, good planning, adequate rehearsal, usable notes and disaster limitation plan. Easy? Certainly not, but by no means impossible, and some of the best speeches I have heard have been given by shy people. If you know that you can deal with your nervousness and stage fright, and that you have a good speech which people will enjoy, what else is there to worry about?

Let's start with the planning and preparation. You have to find out as much as you can about the event you will be speaking at. You need to know who will be there and as much as you can about the venue. You need to know who else will be speaking and what they are going to say. If necessary phone them up and ask them so that your speeches won't overlap. Make sure that you know what your audience will want to hear and at what level you will have to pitch your speech, if it is to have a technical content. Find out how long it should last. Don't be in the least embarrassed about preparing well and ask as many questions as you have to—that's what other people do. Find out what the task is.

Now you have to write your speech. Keep it simple, and cover the areas you will be expected to cover. Thank the right people and remember the bridesmaids if you are speaking at a wedding! Don't try jokes if you aren't experienced. There is nothing worse than a joke which doesn't get a laugh. Tell anecdotes instead, and if your audience likes them they have the option of laughing or smiling. Make the content of your speech interesting. People will listen to any story just to hear the end, but remember that long stories are boring and you don't want to lose your audience. Make sure that your speech has a beginning, a middle, and an end when you pull everything together.

When you have written down what you want to say, read it out loud and time it. Revise what you have written over and over again until it sounds right, and it takes the right length of time. Now you have to rehearse just like any performer. You must record your speech on a tape recorder so that you know what your own voice sounds like. When you stand up and everyone turns towards you, that is the 'crunch' moment when you freeze. Then you must be able to go on auto-pilot. You don't want to be surprised at that moment by the sound of your own voice, so learn your speech, listen to it, and if you have access to a video camera watch your speech, or at least see what you look like in a mirror. You cannot prepare too much.

You have to make notes which you can use on the night. Don't write out the whole speech—you would get lost in a sea of typewriting, and you don't want to read your speech, so you need notes made in big writing with headings underlined so that if you get lost you don't need to panic— you simply look down and pick up the next big underlined heading you see. Make your notes on cards which are handy to use and will fit into your pocket. Make an individual card for your ending, so that if you really want to abort your speech in the middle, or if you overrun and want to go to the end, you simply have to refer to the last card. Your speech will finish perfectly.

Anticipate your problems. You know what you are going to feel like. You know how difficult it may be, so use your relaxation together with your planning to imagine your way though the evening from your arrival to the end of your speech, relaxing away your problems. Speaking is all about confidence, and in your case that means confidence that you have prepared well, that you know your audience and that your speech is as good as you can get it. Know too that everyone is nervous about public speaking, so your audience will be forgiving.

On the night, your main task is to turn up. Getting there can be a problem because of the amount of adrenalin flowing and its physical consequences, but when you turn up you are locked into the organization of the evening and things will go according to plan. As you get near to your speech you won't feel too good, but you won't feel as bad as you expected either. Then there is the embarrassment of the introduction, and you are on your feet. The 'crunch' moment is on you and everything may go blank, but you are prepared for that. Read your first card if you have to and as soon as you can, defuse the situation by making some light-hearted remark or tell an anecdote. Speak slowly, and treat your speech like a conversation using pauses and gambits. Before you know it, your speech will be over and all your laborious preparation will have been worthwhile. There is nothing more gratifying than the knowledge that you have given a satisfactory performance.

The same rules apply to any public performance. If you have to ask a question from the back of the hall, write it down and read it if you get stuck. Prepare as well as you can for any speech, particularly if it's only to the local primary school or the Women's Institute. These little local speeches can be the most difficult and the most disastrous. Think of the potential problems and then expect the unexpected. The chairman may drop dead or you may forget your glasses. Cope with problems as they arise. The interesting thing is that no matter how much you may dread having to make a speech, no matter how ill you may feel beforehand, it is something that you will enjoy on the night and your sense of achievement will be immense.

Take the same systematic approach to the learning of any new skills you may need. Put the effort in beforehand in private, and you will surprise yourself.

Why bother?

You have to bother. If you are going to overcome your shyness you have to do something to broaden your horizons. What you do in the end is up to you—it depends on your friends at the time and the interests you have. If you have been working to develop new skills, use them. You must break out of the shell your shyness has made for you. Not only can you improve your performance in things you are involved in already, but you can progress from that, and by discovering new interests you can lead a fuller, more stimulating life. If you do take on new activities, they will help you develop better skills to manage the ones you are already involved in, at work, for example. You have to keep moving on, particularly if you want to make new friends; you have to meet new people to find new sources of friends. So for your own sake, you have to bother.

REMEMBER:

- You have learned new skills, so you should use them.
- Using these skills means expanding your horizons.
- You have to actively seek new friends and new experiences.
- Find something which you really want to pursue.
- Use it as a tool to continue your fight against your shyness.
- You can learn how to be a competent public speaker.

Chapter 10

Adolescence

It is possible to be shy as a child, it is possible to be shy in later life, but the time when shyness seems worst is in our teens. That's when shyness really matters, when we are at our most vulnerable. That's when it hurts most. It is in our teens that we desperately want to be able to do something about our shyness, and it is the time when we should do something about our shyness. We have every right to enjoy our younger years, and if they are marred by excessive shyness we can't get them back and live them again. They are lost forever, and that should not be.

If you are in your teens and you are shy, everything that has been said in this book so far applies to you too. You really do have to do the exercises and to work on your confidence, but it may be particularly difficult for you for various reasons. Adolescence is such an important time that it merits a chapter to itself.

Why are our teens different?

There are all sorts of factors which make our teens different and therefore difficult. Some are obvious, and some not so obvious. Clearly it is a time in our lives when many things are new, where there are new problems to be solved and new difficulties to be faced. As we get older we become more adept at solving these psychological problems, or perhaps it is just that we disguise them better, so that we can fool other people that we are managing and we can even fool ourselves. In our teens we have still to learn those skills.

In our teens we are also experiencing great changes, not just in our bodies as they mature, but also in our minds. Our ambitions alter, the things we want out of life, and our emotions also become less predictable. It can be difficult for anyone, but for a shy person it is worse. If you are shy you perhaps didn't really know it until you entered your teens, but with the dawn of adolescence the problems become acute and the frustrations unmanageable. Then there is the problem of having to come to terms with your sexuality, and that is the most difficult problem of all.

Sexual maturity

In adolescence your body goes from being that of a child to being that of a sexually mature adult. It is a huge change, not just in physical terms, but also in the demands it puts upon the emotions and psychology. It creates all kinds of conflicting feelings and not a few worries. Some people might feel that a detailed discussion of the sexual hang-ups of adolescents would be embarrassing, but that isn't the case. Embarrassment comes when things aren't discussed, when young people get the wrong ideas and develop problems which may last for their entire lives. It's important to get adolescence right, not just for the future, but because it is a potentially happy time of our lives which we can't relive. You only get one chance.

Everyone has heard that schooldays are the happiest days of your life, but no one believes it, at least not when they are at school. It might just as easily be said that adolescence is the happiest time of one's life, and I doubt if anyone would believe that when they are young. Yet in your teens you have few responsibilities and a great freedom to do the things you want to do without always having to think of the consequences. You have no one else to worry about apart from yourself, and best of all there is the possibility of excitement: there are new experiences to be enjoyed, new battles to fight and new friends of both sexes to make. That is fine if you aren't shy. If you are shy it can be miserable.

Why be miserable?

If you are a shy child you may well become a shy teenager, or you may have no idea that you are shy, so that it comes as a surprise when you find certain things difficult. There are some aspects of our lives which we handle less well than others. You might be very good at sports, or very competent academically, and that may seem to be enough. Life is full and you are flying high, until you notice that your friends have got girlfriends or boyfriends, or that everyone else seems to have a better social life than you, and the things that you are so good at just don't seem important any more. You may try to compete, but life has moved into a new phase and you have been left behind.

You just have to get this sorted out. You can't afford to miss the boat, and that means that you have to sort out your shyness. There is no need for you to be miserable, but if you are going to enjoy your teens you will have to do some work, and much of that work has already been outlined in previous chapters. The first thing to do is to decide that you simply aren't going to be miserable, that you are going to do something about it, and then just knuckle down to the tasks which will allow you to enjoy your teens.

There are however, some particular difficulties which occur in your teens and they are to do with the fraught area of sex. You have to sort them out, but this kind of hang-up cannot be separated from the other problems which any shy person might experience. All sorts of factors operate together to create traps for young people, and we will consider all of them.

Adolescent psychology

Young people go through phases. They feel different things at different times as they are growing up, and in the first phase they tend to stick together in single-sex groups: butch bunches of boys and giggles of girls. Boys and girls are, of course, aware of each other, they are aware of sexual attraction, they may talk about each other, but by and large they avoid direct contact with each other.

There is another factor in the psychology of the young person, and that is the desire to conform. Young people almost dress in a uniform—the particular uniform may vary wildly between groups of teenagers, but it is a uniform nonetheless—and they will do anything to avoid being conspicuous within their own circle. Why should they feel like that? Well, in the last chapter we made some mention of group psychology, and how it gives a person an identity and a strength to be a member of a group. It can give security and support; it can even give permission for ideas and feelings. When a young person is heading out into the uncharted and dangerous world of adulthood, a group is a very comfortable place to be. This is often even more true for boys than for girls.

If you are shy you may do very well in a group. If that is so you are lucky, because being part of a group is an essential first step in the adult world. If you are so shy that you can't function in a group, or if you have been unlucky enough not to make friends of your own sex because you have moved house or something like that, the next stage can be more difficult.

Starting off

The first thing you have to do if you are young is to learn how to relate to others of your own sex. If you have the security of a group you will find it easier to relate to others of the opposite sex. Young people are luckier now than they were in previous generations when everyone was more reserved than they are in the present day. This applies to society as a whole, and now that sex is talked about openly it has lost much of its mystique and is less threatening. Groups of friends now often consist of members of both sexes, and relationships are much less formal. If you go to a single-sex school your friends will naturally be of your own sex, but there are opportunities outside school which didn't exist before. Just to take one example, Boy Scouts used to be for boys and Girl Guides for girls, but now Ranger Guides and Venture Scouts have a sophisticated social life which cuts across sexual borders. There has been a revolution in the social life of young people and there are fewer taboos than there used to be.

If you haven't got a satisfactory social life, and you are a young person, you should take steps to make one using the techniques which have been discussed elsewhere in this book. You can't afford to write off social life as something which doesn't matter. It does matter because, apart from the fact that it is enjoyable for its own sake, out of this type of group social activity comes the stage of getting girlfriends or boyfriends, and of course that leads on to steady relationships. Even if this prospect is so remote that you can hardly contemplate it, it is one of the most important things in life, so you must make the effort to get it right now because you won't be a teenager for ever! You owe it to yourself.

For the moment you won't be thinking about the future, you will be interested in enjoying yourself and in the excitement of making new friends and new experiences. There may be aspects of this new life which frankly frighten you, and there may be aspects of the changes in yourself which frighten or perplex you.

Changes

Physical changes and psychological changes go hand in hand as they always do. In adolescence changes of both types are profound, and they can be disturbing. The physical changes in both sexes are obvious, and as schools nowadays usually provide comprehensive sex education, most people understand very well what these changes are and why they happen. What isn't so easy is coming to terms with the results. In simple terms we develop an interest in members of the opposite sex, but that is an over-simplification. What we also develop is a burning physical interest in sex itself, and to many young and sensitive people that seems wrong. Sex in this form seems dirty and unacceptable, and it is hard to see how it fits in with the genuine admiration for the individuals of the opposite sex with whom we relate. These powerful sensations may cause us to feel guilty, and they can be a bar to the development of normal relationships.

Girls tend to know all about periods and reproduction, and they seem to be able to accept the physical changes which occur with more ease than boys do, perhaps because their problems are discussed more openly amongst women and with their friends, or because they have a better relationship with their mothers, and can discuss these problems at home. Boys are expected to be macho and self-sufficient, and are not meant to have the dreadful self-doubts which a sensitive or shy person can have, and it is unlikely that they discuss their sexual development with their fathers or their friends in a meaningful way. There is no one to give them permission for the feelings they have, and there is no one to tell them that the physical experiences they may have are normal. They experience penile erections which wake them from sleep, and worse, nocturnal emissions (wet dreams) which come without any bidding from them. Sex is thrust upon them, and if they are not prepared mentally it can be very distressing and may lead to terrible feelings of guilt.

This type of physical awareness of sex leads naturally on to masturbation, once a dirty word but now accepted as something very normal, especially in young boys. It is, after all, just about impossible to ignore an erect penis, particularly if it is your own. Masturbation is a perfectly normal part of sexuality. It is a phase you go through until it is replaced by something more adult, and nothing more than that, but it can also be very disturbing if the boy doesn't understand it or feels guilty about it.

Girls also have a world of sexual fantasies, and may suffer embarrassment from the development of breasts, the most obvious sign of female sexual maturity, or worse, by the non-development of breasts when other girls are developing theirs. Knowing that boys are aware of your breast size and development can be agony, though in modern times breasts have declined in significance as signs of sexuality with the disappearance of the uplift bra. These things are a matter of fashion.

So how can sensitive young people reconcile this world of apparent sexual grubbiness with the real world where girls are pure and boys are nice? The fact is that the real world is very different from the image shy teenagers have of it. Sex is a real part of life, and a necessary, enjoyable and fulfilling one at that.

Reconciling the extremes

You have to sort these problems out if you are to move on into a relaxed mature adult existence, or even if you are to enjoy your own youth. It is here that groups of both sexes can help sort out your feelings. If you know that other boys or girls feel and think the same way as you do, that gives you permission to have those feelings and thoughts. If all the girls talk about boys in a particular way, you can accept that those feelings are allowable. The reverse can also be true. If you are a shy girl and part of a group who all talk about boys and you aren't interested, you feel you have to pretend to be interested, which can make you even more insecure than you are already. But even so, there is strength and security in a group, and you need those things if you are troubled by your desires, sensations and feelings.

So far we have been talking about private things, but there comes a time when you will want to meet and get to know members of the opposite sex. You may know lots of girls and boys and be comfortable with them, but that isn't what I mean. Shyness really strikes you down when you have to form a one-to-one relationship, even if that is only for an evening. Doing that can be the most terrifying thing that anyone ever has to do. A brash confident young man or woman wouldn't understand—they probably can't even see the problem, but for a shy person everything about sexual relationships at even the most superficial level is difficult.

The problems

There are all sorts of problems you can have. You have your normal shyness of course, the difficulty in making conversation, the fear of long silences, simply not knowing what to say or do. On top of that is the knowledge that you

are being judged sexually, something entirely new. You
don't know what is required, you don't know how to react,
and you are scared of what you might feel. Most of all, you
are scared of rejection or of being inadequate in some way.
It is the first time in your life where you may be rejected
physically, where you have to put your whole self on the
line and hold nothing back.

A shy person always feels insecure, and the young shy
person feels doubly insecure. There are the usual doubts
about dress, about not wanting to feel different, not wanting
to feel rejected, and then there are the doubts about sexual
adequacy. Even the smallest acts of intimacy, even the leg-
endary stolen kiss, are fraught with problems. Quite simply,
how do you do it, will you be good at it, will the girl or the
boy secretly laugh at you and go back and tell their friends
how inadequate you were? Sometimes it is almost too difficult to contemplate.

The main problem is the eternal one of not being able to
let your guard down. Shy people are too fragile, too vulnerable, have an ego so easily damaged that they will not
hazard themselves. They simply cannot relax with someone
of the opposite sex, and may be aware during a date that
they are making fools of themselves by talking pompous
rubbish, or at least not doing themselves justice, but
because of their shyness they can do nothing about it.
Given time they would relax, but they may not get a second chance.

This fear of rejection, of making a fool of themselves, can
be disastrous. It can be impossible, physically and completely
impossible, for a shy boy to pluck up enough courage to ask
a girl out. The girl may be dying to be asked out, but that
makes no difference to the shy boy. Many a perfect match
has never been made because of shyness. All young people
are a bit shy, and it is common for girls and boys to use a
friend as a 'broker', or often a series of friends of friends, to
arrange a date. It is the group phenomenon again.

There can be greater problems. If you are extremely shy
you might even come to think that there is something
physically or mentally wrong with you, particularly something
of a sexual nature. You might come to believe that some

things which are really natural are unnatural and unacceptable, and it is possible to develop real psychological problems. These particular hang-ups aren't as serious as they seem, and are usually just an expression of other real worries. If you ever feel worried about anything like that you should talk to someone about it. Ideally that person should be a parent, but it could be a doctor or some adult you know and trust. Don't let things like that prey on your mind.

Why does it happen?

Adolescence is difficult for everyone, but it is more difficult for the shy person. A shy person has unrealistic ideas about him- or herself. Shy people may think that they are unattractive, or they may think that their sexual thoughts or practices are disgusting, or they may think that sex itself is disgusting in all its forms. In this they are almost certainly wrong, but such ideas can be deep-seated. More probably they just see themselves as being inadequate compared with all those other people. They just can't compete with the boys who can charm girls, or the girls who have a queue of would-be boyfriends. Their image of themselves is distorted by their shyness, and they cannot do themselves justice. They keep their supposed inadequacies covered up, not realizing that if they just acted naturally they would be as attractive and as sought after as anyone else.

What might be even worse than having a distorted image of one's self is having a distorted image of the opposite sex. If you haven't had many friends of the opposite sex, girls can come to think of boys as being filthy-minded, interested in physical sex only, or boys may think of girls as being unapproachable, or of being likely to tell tales of supposed inadequacies to their friends. It can be hard to match your ideas about sex itself with your thoughts about individual members of the opposite sex, and the result is confusion. It is hard to get over these prejudices, even if you know deep down that they aren't really true, and they can make normal relationships very difficult.

What can you do?

You owe it to yourself to beat the problems of adolescence, but you can't do it by just pulling yourself together. There are a few things that you can do though, to improve your attitude, to adjust your thinking so that you can lead a fuller life.

Firstly, sex is very important in adolescence. Sex is very important in adult life, and that is for good reason. When you first become aware of your own sexuality you have very mixed feelings. You are proud and excited about reaching adulthood, but you are also aware that you are entering uncharted waters, and you have no idea what will be expected of you. Then there are those aspects of your sexuality which may seem unpleasant, even frightening, possibly disgusting. You will have thoughts and ideas which you would rather not have.

All of these things are part of sex. The sexual drive is powerful, a basic part of our being and essential to the continuation of the species. It is important as eating or breathing, and it has many different aspects. Ultimately it is the essence of the relationship between a man and a woman. You have to accept it. You have to accept the thoughts and ideas you may have about it because after all you can't control what you think about. You can't stop yourself from being self-conscious about your sexual development, but you can tell yourself that it is normal and accept that many young people are self-conscious, and that it is normal.

Don't get too serious about sex. Sex is also for fun, and sex is enjoyable. If it wasn't, the human race would have died out. You should enjoy the company of a girlfriend or boyfriend, and you have to practise forming relationships and interrelating if you are going to be able to choose someone with whom you can spend the rest of your life. And you have to learn how much physical contact is possible and acceptable for you, and just how far you can go in a relationship which can be anything from a one-night stand to a lasting partnership. Adolescence is a learning experience.

The cornerstone

There is one guideline which will help you, and that is the fact that any relationship is based upon respect and trust. If you go out with a girl or a boy, whether you have known them before or not, you have to respect them, respect their body and their ideas and values. That is the cornerstone of any relationship. That mutual respect admits all sorts of possibilities in a relationship, including the ultimate experience, that of falling in love and dedicating your life to one person.

It permits other things too, things like affection and the comfort of physical contact with a boyfriend or girlfriend. You have to trust the person you are with, and you have to exercise judgement and sometimes restraint. These are all things that you have to learn, and of course you will make mistakes. There is always the possibility that you will get it wrong, and here lies the main difficulty for the shy person.

Overcoming the problems

The main problem for all shy people of any age is this feeling of vulnerability, and the need to protect oneself against humiliation and embarrassment. Adolescence is all about experiment, and an ability to hazard oneself is a prerequisite. It seems like an impossible situation for a shy girl or boy. How can you solve the problems?

You will have made a start if you can adopt a simple acceptance of the different aspects of your own sexuality, and know that your sexuality is entirely normal both physically and psychologically. If nothing that I have said here can convince you of that, you must seek help from either a parent or someone else that you trust. If you can accept that you are a normal, albeit shy, person, you only have to overcome the problems caused by your shyness. These are the same problems any shy person will have, but the situations you meet in adolescence are difficult, and you meet them for the first time without the benefit of experience.

If you are to have girlfriends or boyfriends, you must have the courage to make dates and seek the company of members of the opposite sex. Remember that girls or boys aren't different from yourself in most respects, and that members of the opposite sex are probably going to be considerate and warm-hearted, and that they are just as likely to want to go on a date with you as you are with them. Everyone is looking for the same thing, someone sympathetic with whom they can spend time and learn about life, and if possible enjoy themselves. You must give other people the opportunity to do that with you.

Make sure that your friends are being helpful. Friends of your own sex can be useful in making introductions for you and if your nerve fails at the crucial time they can give you advice and help. Friends can be competitive and sometimes quite malicious if they are immature, so you have to be careful in your choice of friends and confidants. The right friends are invaluable. Try to make ordinary friendships with people of the opposite sex as well, as these friendships can be useful in facilitating liaisons, and the more relaxed you can be with friends of the opposite sex, the more fulfilling one-to-one relationships will be.

After adolescence

Life is a continuous river of events, and after you have overcome the initial problems of adolescence there will be other situations to face. Once you have got used to making relationships with members of the opposite sex, those relationships may become a problem in themselves. It is of course better to have relationships than not to have them, but relationships have to be managed carefully. There is ample scope for mistakes in any situation, and mistakes can be painful in the area of human relationships. How do you know which is the right person for you? How do you know if you are in love, and if you have a steady relationship how far should you go sexually?

It would be nice if the answers to these questions were easy, or if there were simple rules to follow, but alas, there aren't. Some of the most unlikely relationships develop, and they can work very well for reasons which no observer can understand. In this area above all others you have to rely on your own instincts and feelings. There *is* such a thing as love, and anyone who has experienced it will tell you that it is the finest emotion that anyone can feel, and it lasts. It is love that makes everything else right, and shy people have the sensitivity and the compassion to experience love.

If you are apprehensive about having a sexual relationship, if you doubt your ability to manage the sexual side of a relationship, you don't have to worry. You won't be having sex with a stranger, you will be sharing the experience with someone you care about and who cares about you. If that isn't the case, you may be making a mistake. Sex occurs naturally in a caring relationship, and your views about when it should happen will be coloured by your religion, your upbringing and experience and the wishes of your partner. It isn't something you have to worry about, it is a natural occurrence which can heighten a relationship and even change your life. It certainly shouldn't be taken lightly or casually. You will have too much respect for yourself and your body for that.

Lastly, if you seriously think you might be gay or lesbian, take advice about that from the organizations which offer help and advice to gay people. You too deserve a happy adolescence and a happy life, and our society is much more tolerant now than it has been. If you have doubts about your sexuality seek advice—don't be shy.

Relationships require social skills, so all that has been said in this book applies to you if you are an adolescent. You have to work on your confidence in physical ways using all the techniques already described, and you have to apply them in the admittedly very difficult situations you will have to face. You can overcome your problems, but they will be solved mostly by experience, and to get experience you have to do something active. Have courage, and go out and enjoy your adolescence.

REMEMBER:

- Adolescence is difficult for everyone, though it is much worse for a shy person.
- Sex is an important part of life, and you have to learn how to deal with it.
- Accept the unexpected feelings and thoughts you may have about sex and sexual relationships: sex is like that.
- The only way to learn about relationships is to have them, and you learn by experience.
- Members of the opposite sex are approachable, and they have the same values and aspirations as you do.
- Have the courage to make friends and experiment with relationships with boys or girls.

Chapter 11

Scaling the heights

So far in this book we have talked about keeping up with other people who are lucky enough not to be shy. We have been thinking 'Why can't I be as good as he is?' 'Why can't get the boyfriends that she gets?' 'Why can't I get the promotions that he gets? After all, I'm as good as he is!' Our ambition has been simply to emulate the achievements of others, to get by in a difficult world. We have concentrated on purely practical steps which yield practical results, and we have not mentioned changing our attitudes to ourselves or to the world outside. We can do better.

Shy people tend to be pessimistic about their abilities. They see the glass of water as being half empty, and in so doing they underestimate their potential. A shy person is unlikely to ask himself or herself, 'Why can't I be managing director of the company?' Yet is there any reason why that person shouldn't be as ambitious as, or even more ambitious than, anyone else? Shouldn't a shy person wish for even more fulfilment to compensate for the loss experienced just by being shy for all of those years? A shy person apologizes for himself or herself, or at least feels apologetic or inadequate, and lacks confidence, yet a shy person is as able as anyone else and, some might argue, more able than most. We'll come to that later.

A new fact

All this may have been true about you, but there is now a new fact which has to be to be taken into consideration, and now is the time to face that fact. Quite simply:

You aren't shy any more.

That is the new truth. If you have done the exercises, both physical and psychological, and if you have expanded your activities and possibly your circle of friends, you aren't shy any more. That is a very difficult thing to face up to. You no longer have an excuse for not achieving anything you want to achieve. You may be saying to yourself that it isn't really true, that you can still feel shy on occasion, but then most people feel ill at ease part of the time, and everyone feels uncomfortable in some situations. You don't know what they are feeling, and even the most extrovert person may be behaving in a particular way simply to cover up a lack of confidence.

Remember that we said that you would not be able to change your basic personality? Of course you can't, but we have changed a great many things closely related to that personality. It might be that all that's holding you back now is your attitude. You are the sort of person who has had difficulty letting go, and that includes letting go of your inhibitions. It's time to admit that you aren't shy, certainly not the way you were, that your shyness doesn't dominate or limit your life, and ask yourself what you are going to do about it.

Being liberated from your shyness opens up all sorts of possibilities, and you may well have to rethink many of your attitudes to life. Most of all you will have to sort out your aspirations and ambitions in every aspect of your life. If you are young, just about anything is possible. If you are older, you may have fewer options, but there is still much that you can achieve. You have wasted a lot of time just being shy and you have a lot of time to make up.

Measuring progress

If you have made serious efforts to overcome your shyness you will have made progress. That stands to reason. If you have any doubts, do a simple exercise. Let's go back to the notebook and pencil we have more or less abandoned, and write a few notes about what you were like before you started to tackle your shyness. Stick to the practical things first, and make a list of the things that you could not do. Take the everyday things, the things at work or in your social life, the small things that you so easily forget. You are an imaginative person who will be able to summon up those little agonies again, and you can use some of the notes you made when you started to read this book as a guide.

Now do the same for the present day. Take the same sort of situation and think about the way you handle it now. Think about the way you feel, think about the things you are prepared to tackle which you might not have done previously. There will be a difference, a substantial difference and that difference will continue to grow. At the very worst you will be able to see a way forward, a path which you can follow which will lead on to a more confident and fulfilled life. If you haven't yet got down to the exercises, it's time you did.

Changing your attitude

We have done the practical things; now we need to move on. Of course it would be inappropriate to say to a shy person: 'Don't be shy. Change your attitude, pull yourself together, just get on with it.' You have, however, already moved on, and you now have the ability to change your attitude and cope with the results. You will have to begin to look at the way you think about things. You cannot continue to take a negative attitude to the events in your life. You must start to think positively. You must have known that we would get around to this eventually, and now we have, but before doing so we have given you the ammunition which you will need to deal with the results. You don't have to be scared of thinking positively. If you say to yourself: 'I can—and I will', you will know that you can, and what we now have to sort out is the 'will'.

We are talking about fulfilment. If you know that you are capable of being the captain of the ship you won't be happy being the second mate. I believe that you now have the ability to be much more than you were previously, and that doesn't necessarily mean at work: it might mean in the world of sexual relationships or in a sport or hobby. I believe that this is true because as a shy person you have insight into the way other people feel. You are sensitive and you are able, but you have had to contend with tremendous problems, which have held you back like a millstone around your neck. If you can be rid of that millstone you will go a great deal faster, and no hill will be too hard to climb.

You can do better than 'normal' people because just keeping up with 'normal' people has meant a huge effort. Now you have energy to spare. And lastly, you have learned new skills, skills which other people don't have, and you have learned a new attitude which many other people don't have. You have learned to take a detached, analytical approach to problems of all sorts. Any difficulties you might encounter are looked on as being difficulties to be solved. You have techniques which you can use, and you have a new attitude so that you will be able to continue the work you have already done in this book by devising new exercises of your own, new ways of confronting problems and overcoming them.

Doing better

For all of these reasons you can expect to do better, not only than you did before, but better than people with a similar lifestyle and ambitions might expect to do. The only ingredient to add is that of ambition. For many shy people ambition might be a dirty word. Who wants to be ambitious? The answer is that *you* do. Everyone has some ambition in some area of their lives, and often these ambitions are unfulfilled. You may have grand ambitions, political ambitions, professional ambitions, or maybe small personal ambitions, or ambitions for your family. There is nothing wrong with having ambitions.

Ambitions, along with confidence and academic qualifications, are items handed out to students at certain prestigious educational establishments such as British public schools, and added to by some of the great universities. The students are given to believe that they will be at the top of their chosen profession, that they will be captains of industry, generals or judges. At the end of the day they tend to succeed, and their success is due at least in part to the fact that they assume that they will be successful. Attitudes do count. The difference between the achievements of different people is less to do with differences in ability, and more to do with differences in expectation and in attitude. The boy who always gets the most attractive girl isn't necessarily any better-looking than any of his friends—he just has the best attitude.

So attitude does matter, and so far you have been shy and unwilling to make yourself conspicuous, unwilling to push yourself forward or to volunteer. You have been under-estimating yourself and your abilities. Now is the time to break out of this 'shy prison'.

Changing your attitudes

How do you start to make changes in your attitudes? Well, of course it isn't easy. You have already done a lot to change your everyday life and make it more fulfilled and more comfortable, but we are now talking about really making it, really getting to the top. You have to begin to think positively, and if you are to do that you have to con-sider some more exercises. You might have hoped that you had come to the end of this type of thing, and in fact we are nearing the end, but there is one more peak to climb.

Start writing, or talk into a tape recorder if it's easier. Start talking about yourself and your life, maybe under some specific headings to give your ramblings some form. Talk about the way things are, and the things you might want to achieve or be involved in, using headings such as Work, Social Life, Sporting Achievement, Sex Life, Future Projects. Write a few paragraphs about each, and about anything else that comes into your mind. Say how things are going now, how they may go in the future, how you would like them to go and perhaps why they might not go the way you want them to go. Deal with both short-term and long-term objectives. Do it now, before you read any further.

When you have made these few notes, read them back, or listen to them if you have recorded them, and note any negative ideas or inferences you have included. Shy people are full of negative ideas, but you aren't shy any more, so you shouldn't be writing like a shy person. No more 'I might do this...' or, 'I could do this if only....' or, 'I would like to do this but...'

Do the exercise again, but this time no negative ideas are permitted. Write a strong positive statement, whether it seems realistic or not. Simply write a strong positive dissertation about your life now, and the way it's going to be. Don't say, 'I would like to be head of my department in time,' say instead, 'I will be head of the department in three years.' Say, 'I will have a steady boyfriend by Christmas.' Your little essay may be idealized, but do it anyway.

Read that back and see if it seems as fanciful as you thought. Now we can continue with the exercise by writing some more. Don't write about the things that are preventing you from achieving your ambition, write about the things you will have to do to make your ambitions happen. Do it in detail, and make out a timetable for everything you want to achieve. Do it in a matter-of-fact way and see how that sounds. Is it as unrealistic as you thought? Is it achievable at all? The chances are that there are no practical reasons why you can't do most of the things you want to do. The only thing that's stopping you is your attitude.

Positive thinking

You have to think positively. You cannot afford the sort of negative attitudes upon which shyness feeds, so we now have to do something we have done before in this book. We have to raise into the level of our consciousness something which we currently do without noticing. We have to notice when we have a negative thought, and start thinking, saying and doing only those things which are positive. From now on all our glasses will be half full instead of half empty. You simply have to be aware of the way you think about things. You have to notice when you have a negative thought, and when you do notice one, turn it round and think of the alternative positive idea.

The positive diary

You need help in this task, and again the help comes from a pen and paper. It will be useful if you keep a diary for a while, but it has to be a special sort of diary, and one which would not make much sense to anyone else who might read it. It is a diary which contains only positive thoughts. Most diaries contain the writer's uncertainties and doubts, and are full of negative ideas. That's what diaries are usually for, but your positive diary is being kept purely as an exercise and isn't meant to be comprehensive. It will present one side only, the positive side, and you can use it for planning your approach to events you are going to attend and things you are going to achieve.

There's no point at all keeping a positive diary unless you have acquired the skills to implement your positive ideas. You have to be able to relax, to be in control of situations and to have the skills to direct conversation and project your best image. You may have had to learn how to be a bit of an actor so that you don't appear shy to others, but now you expect your diary to start to show you the way to the top. Let's look at the experiences of a young man I once knew.

Peter

Peter was a student when I first knew him. He was studying English, Politics and Economics and although he was exceptionally bright, he seemed to be getting nowhere. His problem wasn't anything to do with his academic ability, it was simply that he was excessively shy so that whilst his friends seemed to be having a ball at the university, he wasn't making new friends and he was uncertain how his life was going to develop. He hadn't joined any societies, he didn't have a girlfriend and he had no idea what he was going to do after he graduated. He was becoming lost.

Peter sounds like a rather dismal and uninteresting person, but he wasn't. He was good-looking, he was very able, and he was sensitive and caring. He had the reputation of being stable and reliable, and friends and acquaintances came to him for advice. They urged him to take part in the life of the university. He was recognized as being shy, and the girls in his year regretted that he didn't mix like most of the other students. Peter desperately wanted to mix, realizing that he was wasting great opportunities, but he was too shy.

Shyness was the problem, but Peter had no idea how he could deal with it and he was running out of time. His friends were all getting more or less permanent girlfriends, and he was stuck in a rut. What could he do?

He began as you might expect, by taking advice and getting on with the nuts and bolts of his shyness, learning the basic lessons about managing his body and developing social skills, but as he rapidly became proficient in these areas he began to think further ahead. It was time to change up a gear and really reap the benefits of all his hard work. He had to not only learn to think positively, he also had to learn to act positively and develop a game plan for the next few weeks, and long-term objectives for the next few years.

Peter was nothing less than determined, and he kept a positive diary as he was advised to do. As you might expect, his attitudes and manner became more positive, and almost without knowing it he began to take more part in the life of the university. He had made a list of the things he wanted to achieve, some of them very personal, and some more general, but how could he realize these ambitions? They wouldn't happen by themselves, which is why he needed a plan.

Other people might have organized these things without any trouble, without having to give them a thought, but Peter was shy and he was lacking in experience, and he had no close friends to advise him. He had two short-term ambitions on his list. One was to advance his social opportunities in the university so that he could get the most benefit from his time there. The second was to find a partner to accompany him to a formal dance which was to be held in a few weeks' time. Of course he wasn't allowed to wonder if these things were achievable or not, he was only permitted to think how they could be achieved.

His first move was to decide to stand for the post of year representative for the university historical society. That took some courage because there was the chance of public rejection, but he worked and canvassed quietly and to his surprise found that he was liked and respected, and he won easily. This opened the doors for all sorts of things. He had to do some public speaking, which was good experience, and he had to attend social functions which was also good experience. The only thing which had been holding him back from a very fulfilled undergraduate life was himself.

And the girlfriend? Not just any girlfriend, but the particular girl he had liked ever since he had arrived at the university. Elaine was quiet but popular, and under normal circumstances nothing would have induced him to ask her out. Now he had to think positively, and it's amazing how the different parts of one's life mesh together. He now had to attend the formal dance as a committee member of the historical society, and so he was a desirable partner, but just the same he had to have someone to go with. If he couldn't approach Elaine himself, how could he ask her out? He had to think positively, so he had to find a way. He couldn't allow himself to wonder if she would accept, he just had to find a way to ask her.

He did some research. He asked who she shared her flat with, and he found that one of his own friends was the boyfriend of one of her flatmates, so he re-invented the teenage trick of using a go-between. He enquired if she had been asked, and in so doing he expressed an interest which he discovered was reciprocated. Then it was a simple matter of arranging the details.

All this sounds very devious, but it is all part and parcel of life, and if it produces results, so much the better. Peter went on to become president of the historical society, and in time he married Elaine, and when it came to realizing his long-term ambition, which was that of getting into a post-graduate course, his undergraduate activities and his natural academic ability made it seem easy. In time, no doubt, he will be a lecturer. He can't put all that down to positive thinking....or can he?

Personal ambitions

The ambitions of a young person are almost straightforward compared with the problems shyness might produce in an older person, or indeed in a younger person with particularly severe problems. As a general rule, as you get older you find ways of disguising your shyness, or of circumnavigating it. Even so, getting older creates problems because an older person usually doesn't have the support of a group of friends. You are on your own, often with no one to talk to. Even if you are married or live with somebody, there can be personal problems or ambitions which you might not wish to discuss with your spouse.

Someone who has problems with his or her sexuality may be too shy to talk about it openly, or maybe even to admit to himself. These are particular problems which require specialist help, and as we have said before when talking about young people in particular, it would be a mistake to be too shy about them to seek such help. Someone with these problems, whatever their age, must take their courage in both hands and make an approach to his or her doctor, who should be able to give advice or refer that person to someone who can help.

Shyness is behind many personal problems involving sexuality which some people, often slightly older people, experience. Such people may be happily married, but the remnants of their hang-ups in adolescence still haunt them. There may be shyness or embarrassment due to misunderstandings about the nature of sexual function. In even the most happy marriage, sexual anxiety can create a barrier between the partners.

This chapter is about scaling the heights, and that doesn't just mean excelling in a career or achieving outstanding ambitions, it means excelling in all areas of one's life, even the most intimate. It means living life to the full, getting the best out of life and out of one's relationships, and it might even mean doing better than other people and achieving more than other people might achieve in all areas of life, including sex.

Sex is a means of establishing and maintaining a loving relationship, but it should be more than that. Sex can mean all sorts of things. It can and should be fun, and on other occasions it can be a way of expressing tenderness. It should be a way of showing respect, but it can also on occasions be exciting and different. It can push back the frontiers of a relationship and make it deeper and more meaningful. How can sex fulfil all of these different and apparently conflicting tasks? I doubt if anyone can answer that question.

It's not easy to explain why experimenting with sex, by trying new and different forms of sex, can deepen a relationship, but it can. The probable explanation is that sex is a deep and primeval instinct and that many people have sexual fantasies which they cannot explain rationally even to themselves. By sharing them with a partner they expose a very personal and private part of themselves, and providing their partner understands and shares their aspirations, something very important can happen to their relationship. It is however, an area which shy people often find difficult.

It can be difficult for a shy person to discuss sexual problems even with a partner of many years. You don't want to risk causing offence or embarrassment, or you might just not wish to appear foolish, yet opportunities might be lost and worse, relationships can get into difficulty due to pure boredom, and there is the risk of infidelity if one partner isn't satisfied with the sexual side of the relationship. Of course these arguments should never be used to force one partner to indulge in any sexual act which he or she does not willingly consent to, but it is an argument for discussing the options. These discussions could be initiated by either partner. A wife may, for example, not be achieving orgasms as often as her husband, so they might simply discuss the techniques they can use to remedy this. The important thing for a shy person is to feel that these matters can be discussed. If there are problems, there are plenty of very respectable books available which can help a couple deal with their difficulties. If you have problems initiating such a discussion, you could ask your partner to read the preceding paragraphs.

Other ambitions

What about other ambitions? We are talking about scaling the heights, of doing better than the average person. If you have the ambition, you have the skills. You have developed a technique which involves studying a problem in detail and looking at the intricate mechanics of both your reaction and those of the other people involved. You will be used to writing things down and simplifying the haphazard method of problem solving by developing a plan tailored to your needs. You are miles ahead of most people as they stumble through life, and you should be geared up for success at whatever you choose to tackle. You have every right to assume that you can succeed.

One of your problems is to decide what you want out of life. It can be very difficult, but you have plenty of time and many avenues to explore. Take your time and progress slowly. If, for example, you enjoy public speaking and being involved in public life, you can join the political party of your choice and test the water. You may start by delivering leaflets, but if you have any potential and can speak in public you will find that that sort of person is in short supply and you will soon be asked to put yourself forward as a candidate, possibly in local government. You may never have realized that candidates for all parties are sometimes in very short supply and you could even end up being elected to high office.

If you join a club there is always a demand for people to become organizational committee members. People don't like to put themselves forward, yet being on a committee can be fun. It is good to be involved.

Making major changes

What should you do if your life is really very unsatisfactory? What if your work is a bore, if your sex life is unfulfilling or worse, absent altogether? What if you just can't see the future clearly and don't know what to do? Should you consider making major changes in your life in the hope of finding a more satisfactory lifestyle?

We have asked a lot of questions and the answers aren't easy to find, but one thing is absolutely certain: you have to proceed with the greatest caution. You can't answer all of your questions at once, so if you're really sure that you want to make changes you have to take the same systematic approach that you have taken to other problems. If you are really dissatisfied with your life, first of all you have to find out why. You may think you know why your life is unsatisfactory, but if you are determined to make major changes it is imperative that you make the right ones, because it may be impossible to turn the clock back after you have made a change.

The sort of thing we are thinking about is leaving home, changing your job, moving to another area, taking the opportunity of a job abroad, getting divorced or leaving your partner. These are major decisions which need a lot of thought. If you are sure that some change is needed in your life, you have to decide what you should do, and again a paper and pencil will help you to be logical. Of course not all decisions are logical, but you have to give yourself the opportunity to be logical, to see all the options and to work out the consequences. If you then follow your instincts and do the thing you first thought of that's fine, but you will at least know what you are letting yourself in for.

Making changes isn't often the answer to problems. At the end of the day you may have changed your situation, but you are still the same person with the same problems. You would be much better doing the things discussed in this book and making yourself as proficient as possible in the situation you are in now. Let's assume that you have done that, and parts of your life are still a disaster—what should you do? Let's assume that you just can't stand your job, that work is terrible and that your dislike of it is nothing to do with your shyness, it's just that you can't stand your job any more. The same might be true of your home situation, or even of your social life, especially if you live in a remote place. You might feel that you want to change your situation. How do you make these decisions?

Playing consequences

Once again, what we have to do is write things down. Begin by making a list of the things in your life which you can change. Record everything, no matter how small and insignificant, and include the major changes too. When you have made an exhaustive list, take the most promising change and write that at the top of a page. Now you should write down a list of the advantages which might result from that change, and again nothing is too insignificant to record. When you have your list go back to the beginning and take your first conclusion a step further. Ask yourself 'What would happen if...':

'If I leave home, I will have more freedom. If I have more freedom I can bring friends home. My mother won't always be watching and commenting about how often I go out and the time I come home at. I will have a more relaxed social life. I will be able to do more, to go more places, and have boyfriends/girlfriends. I will be able to have an active sex life. I will be able to form more stable relationships and lead a more adult life.'

Do this for all of your options, and see where it leads you, and then unfortunately you have to record the negative side, and list all the disadvantages and pursue each to its logical conclusion. After all this work you should have some sort of idea as to what is likely to happen as a result of any decision, and you will have a feel as to what may be the right thing to do.

If you are going to make major changes in your life make them because you want to, because your life needs those changes, and not because you are shy. It's like getting fit to play squash instead of making the error of taking up squash to get fit and so killing yourself. Overcome your shyness so that you can make and deal with changes in your life, don't make the changes to deal with your shyness. That simply doesn't work.

Be ambitious

You must let your ambitions have full rein. If you don't you will lead a life of frustration. You can achieve the things that other people achieve, but you can do better than that. You can be a leader of society. Don't ask yourself why; ask yourself why not?

REMEMBER:

- Don't allow yourself to have negative thoughts: think positively.
- Keep a positive diary and use it to help you to fulfil your ambitions, both personal and private.
- If you join a club or take part in any organization, consider taking a leading role: other people prefer to take a back seat and you do have the ability.
- Don't make changes in your life to overcome your shyness. Only make changes when your shyness is under control.

Chapter 12

Getting there

Living with shyness is a struggle. Anything is more difficult for the shy person than it is for someone who isn't shy. It is hard for someone who isn't shy to know what it's like to be shy, to understand what a handicap it is. It can be as difficult for a shy person to attend a dinner party as it might be for a non-shy person to speak at a national conference. Yet a shy person does have a few advantages over the non-shy person. He or she is used to dealing with feelings of panic and stress and managing physical symptoms, and as even ordinary events are difficult, extraordinary events are not necessarily that much more difficult and so there's no reason why you shouldn't go on to tackle major public events. If you are shy and you can manage your shyness, you can become competent at all levels of activity and if you add a dash of ambition, the world can be yours. Many shy people are very successful at all levels of society.

Public life

Exposing your problem to the test of an audience, which is what we all have to do, isn't easy, but then public speaking or appearing at public or social events isn't easy for anyone, and as long as you have the courage to do it, don't worry about the skill you will need because you have already learned it. Over the years you may well have taken refuge in the pursuit of excellence, so that when you do appear in public you do it to perfection with good preparation and

good notes. When you give a presentation you are well prepared and so, in spite of your shyness, you will be good at it.

Private life

If you are shy and lonely, it is difficult to believe that
shyness can be an advantage in life, but it is true. If a shy
person forms a relationship, it will be sincere and true.

Shyness is an attractive attribute. It is a mistake to think
that the only people who are sought after are those who are
hugely attractive, successful and able. Those people can be
intimidating, and we are loved for our faults and our weaknesses as much as for our strengths. If you are shy, above
all else follow the advice in this book and give others the
opportunity to get to know you and to learn to love you.
Don't cut yourself off, either by withdrawing from society or
by forming a psychological wall around yourself. This is an
age when walls are pulled down.

Misapprehensions

If you are shy you may have a slightly distorted view of the
world, a view warped by the fact that it is always seen
through eyes clouded by that ever-present shyness. You
might see yourself as being less able than you are, or less
attractive, and you will see other people as being relatively
more attractive and more able. You will see tasks as more
formidable than they are, and see other people as being
more competent to complete them. You aren't the only one
to have misapprehensions: everyone has them, and we all
read the world in a very subjective way. I will tell you
about Angela, a girl I once knew.

Angela

When I was a student there was a girl who ate in the refectory most evenings. She was quite stunning, and so beautiful that when she came in a silence fell over the entire
room, and she attracted every eye. It happened every night
and the effect was so obvious that it became embarrassing.

In fact Angela wasn't particularly beautiful in a classical sense, but she had a fragile quality which made people notice her. Indeed, it was impossible to ignore her.

It is fair to say that any boy in the hall, or in the university for that matter, would have given almost anything to have had the opportunity of taking her out, but very few ever did. It was much later when I got to know Angela that I discovered to my amazement that she was very shy, and very lonely. She was so attractive that she was unapproachable, and the only men who asked her out were the very ones she didn't want to know. The regular diners in the refectory thought that she too good for them, and that she preferred the company of the pushy unpleasant boys that she did appear with occasionally. What Angela would have liked more than anything was the company of one of the ordinary boys who found her so unattainable, but the barrier of her shyness and their diffidence prohibited any such contact.

I learned several lessons from this experience. Firstly, sexual attractiveness has little to do with good looks, and a great deal to do with image. Angela wasn't a classic beauty, and she wasn't even very confident, but she radiated sexual attractiveness. No one could really explain why, but some of the most sought-after women in the world, such as Marilyn Monroe, have had this combination of physical presence and vulnerability. It is also true that if you think that you have sex appeal, regardless of your physical attributes, then that is what you radiate and that is the message which is received. If you think, dress and behave like someone who is attractive and accessible, then you will have boyfriends. Angela could have learned to appear less remote.

The same is true in other situations. I remember talking to a very important and well-known professor one day and noticing that he was rather short, whereas I had always thought that he was tall. He had a tremendous presence, and one naturally attributed to him physical characteristics he didn't have. We are back to the discussion of image again, the subconscious transmission of information by body language. It isn't even to do with confidence, more to do with the way we think about ourselves. We can't transmit a deliberately false image, but we can change the way we think about ourselves and it might be surprising what could happen.

Looking at the world

Don't take the world at face value. Try to look beyond the obvious and consider why things seem to be the way they are. Remember Angela, whom everyone thought preferred pushy boys. The opposite was true, and it is the same for many attractive girls. If you are a boy you can't complain that the creeps always get the best girls, or that the most interesting girls ignore you. When did you give a girl like that a chance to get to know you? If you are a girl, and you never meet the right kind of boy, do you wonder why? Do you make the effort to get to know a wide range of friends?

In a work situation, if one individual seems to be preferred, take the boss's point of view and see the situation through his or her eyes. Does that individual make more of an effort to present his or her point of view than you do? You can't complain that you don't win if you won't play the game. We aren't talking about 'lifemanship', of assuming a false position, but simply of making the best of ourselves.

You have to learn from these exercises, and you have to be prepared to change. You can't change firmly-held opinions, but you can present your ideas more successfully. If, for example, you aren't able to put your point of view to the boss and everyone else can, because you eat out and they all eat in the staff canteen, that is something you can change. If you are eating in the pub because you are too shy to eat with the boss, then you will have to use your new expertise to overcome that difficulty.

Using a system

When you have taken on the nuts and bolts of your shyness, it helps if you develop a system. You have to find a way of dealing with the world so that you can minimize the effects of your shyness, and we have looked at that in detail, usually with the help of a pen and paper. You are getting to the end of this book now and you have to go forward from here. When you meet a problem you can't solve, ask yourself why. Develop a way of thinking about it so that you can understand it, and then think of a way of overcoming your difficulties. This applies to personal problems and to problems at work; in fact, it applies to all problems. There is a way around any difficulty. Developing a systematic way of thinking about problems is the key to success.

You can use a systematic way of thinking to help you make the major decisions of your life. Of course, the really big decisions of your life are made by instinct. The choice of the person you marry or the car you buy is a matter of personal prejudice, but below this important level of activity there are many decisions which seem to be too difficult to make until you employ a system. This applies to everyone, but a system is particularly helpful for the shy person because the fact of your shyness complicates any decision making.

Decision making

In anyone's life there are major decisions which have to be made. These decisions may affect the rest of your life and may involve employment or career, marriage, or where you live. It would be unfair to pretend that making this type of major decision is easy, or can be made much easier by simple techniques. Such decisions have a great input from your emotions and your experience, and you have to let these facets of your personality play their part. You have overcome much of your shyness and in practical terms you may be on a par with everyone else, but your basic personality is still the same, and your diffidence may still play a part in your decision making.

At the end of the day you can't be someone that you aren't, and you shouldn't pretend to be. In important decision making you have to obey your instincts, and your instincts won't let you down. If your basic personality suggests that you aren't going to be a general in the army, or a TV newsreader, the captain of a ship or a captain of industry, then don't feel that you cannot lead a fulfilled life doing something else. Whatever decisions you take, it is important that your shyness doesn't intrude and dominate your life, and that is why real fulfilment depends on you taking on your shyness at whatever age you may be, tackling it aggressively, and then enjoying the resulting liberation.

The complete person

We have been talking a great deal about shyness as if shyness existed as an entity in itself, somehow removed from the rest of your personality. Shyness is in the end only part of yourself, and though it may be a large part and something which restricts your life, there is much more to you than your shyness. We are all complete people with different talents and different skills, and we all have our part to play. Dealing with shyness is important only because it will let the other parts of yourself out. If you are shy you must deal with your shyness: life is too short to suffer that sort of agony. But what comes now; what happens after you have dealt with the scourge of shyness?

We have talked about scaling the heights in your work activities and even in the intimate parts of your personal life, but that was just a consideration of the options open to you now that you are no longer shy. You should continue to push at doors that seem to be only just ajar. One way to start is to develop new skills not related to your shyness or lack of it. One area might be in sport.

You don't have to be an Olympic medal winner—if you yourself are satisfied with your sporting performance you will be content. Try to get fit and to be fit—you will feel better. Try to develop your knowledge by starting to read, by going to evening classes or by getting into part-time higher education. You will develop a new respect for yourself. Try to expand your life by thinking laterally about the things you might be doing. What you are aiming at is not the pursuit of excellence in any particular area, it is the development of a well-rounded personality. You have an advantage over other people because you have developed a particularly valuable asset. You have developed insight.

Insight

As a shy person you may well have been introspective, possibly too introspective for your own good. That isn't a good thing, and you may have spent much of your time absorbed in yourself to the exclusion of other interests. Insight is different. If you have insight you have under-standing, you know why things happen, why they may have gone wrong and often what you can do to make them right. You know what you think and feel, and as a result you know what motivates other people. In a word, you have wisdom.

Much of this book has been involved in an effort to raise to a conscious level thoughts, feelings, emotions and physi-cal sensations which occur subconsciously to other people. You have become 'tuned in' to the messages of your own body, usually so that you can do something about these phenomena when they go wrong. If you get too tense you should be the first to know. If you overbreathe you should know all about it, if you sweat at a party because of the heat, you should know that *that* is why you feel uncomfort-able. Likewise, if you have personal problems at work, you should be able to work out why that is, why meetings are difficult, or why and how an individual seems to make your life difficult. Gather all this together and you have some-thing called insight, a special knowledge of the mechanisms governing the events occurring around you. This is a spin-off from the efforts you have been making to control your shyness, but it is a valuable asset.

Many people go through life never really understanding what is happening to them. You do understand, and that is why it isn't unreasonable to say, as we have before, that you may be able to do better in the world than people who aren't, or who haven't been, shy. You have discovered insight. People will come to you to find out why certain things are happening to them, to ask what is going on in the office or why an individual is behaving in a certain way. You have not only trained yourself to understand yourself, you have trained yourself to watch others around you and to try to understand what motivates them, and why they behave the way they do. You should be able to use your insight to your own advantage.

Insight is the sort of management skill that people would give their eye teeth to obtain, and if you have it, quietly use it. Use it to help keep yourself on top of the situation, to keep your shyness under control, but take it further than that. Use it to help you understand others so that you can relate better to them and help them to relate to each other, but also use it to get ahead of the game. Your shyness has held you back for years, but if you have insight it can help you anticipate the way events will develop, and that can do you no harm. You can and should do better than other people.

When the going gets tough....

You know the saying: 'When the going gets tough, the tough get going!'

It doesn't say 'when the going gets tough the shy get going'. Shy people are the sort of people who get sand kicked in their faces; or are they? That's one of the illusions about shyness, the idea that somehow being shy is the same as being a wimp. That isn't true: shyness is an affliction and to survive it you have to be tough, you have to be resilient and you have to be a fighter. You don't have to be a brash loudmouth—that's different. You have to have a quiet strength, but don't let a shy person's insight and respect for others stop you from getting tough when you have to. If you see injustice, particularly injustice against you, then it's time you did get going and did something about it.

Of course, complaining about an injustice or demanding a pay rise isn't easy. As a shy person you will have problems with the physical situation and that is something you will have to manage, but you will never back away from making these decisions. When the chips are down, you are as tough as anyone else and probably tougher. In your relationships too, particularly those with the opposite sex, you can be as determined as anyone else, and you should be. In important situations, there's no benefit in saying 'After you.' All's fair in love and war, and in the promotion race and in everything else. When you get your act together, be prepared to stand up for yourself when the need arises and for the sake of your own self respect, make very sure that no one takes advantage of you. Like so many other things, it is something you can practise.

What now?

Dealing with your shyness is a process which has a beginning, a middle, but no end. The advice in this book is meant to be taken in the order it is given because the different techniques mesh one with another. You have to be systematic, start at the beginning and carry on to the....well, is there an end? Is the rest of your life going to be a battle against shyness or can we really say, as we have suggested, that at some stage we have finally and completely defeated our shyness? What do you think?

I wonder if anyone ever completely defeats something as basic as shyness. It is a monster, and when you knock it down you have to keep your foot on its throat. Never give it a chance to leap up and engulf you. The great thing about taking on your shyness is that your own monster gets weaker the longer it is down, so that the effort of keeping it at bay becomes less demanding and uses up less of your time and energy. The important thing is to make a start, to get your monster under control, and then keep it in its place.

That all sounds very easy, but there are pitfalls along the way, and the worst and most common is that of backsliding, of losing interest, of getting discouraged and as a result letting things slip. You simply cannot afford to do that. You have to persevere, even in the face of difficulty, and make sure that you actually do the exercises and use the techniques outlined in this book. Not only that, you have to do them in the order they are listed so that you can build on your successes. Confidence breeds confidence. Take them as a whole, and don't try to implement them piecemeal.

As you go forward from here, keep developing the principles according to your needs, continuing to work on

physical relaxation and on the psychological release of the
constraints of your shyness. Don't be discouraged and don't
give up. As you go along keep in your mind the vision of
yourself as a person released from shyness, know what you
can be and work towards that. Keep that long-term view in
your mind during the reversals which are part of any programme of self-improvement.

Involving others

Everyone needs friends, and friends are important,
particularly for the young. Friends can be a great help, but
they can also cause problems. If your group of friends is
too close, the group can develop an identity of its own,
which can exclude others and inhibit your efforts to
improve yourself. If your friends are shy, they may benefit
from the techniques outlined in this book and having company along the road to overcoming your shyness can be
useful, but in the final analysis you have to help yourself,
and you have to rely on yourself. You may have to enlarge
your group of friends, or to introduce new members to the
group if the group is too introspective and too protective.

If you are short of friends, find ways of making friends by
enlarging your social life, but remember that as a shy person sooner or later you will have to branch out on your
own, and it is then that the inner resources you have been
developing will be required.

The future

There is one good thing to look forward to with increasing
age, and that is something which everyone experiences. As
we get older we develop ways of dealing with our shyness,
whether we plan to or not. You cannot get older without
gaining in experience, and with experience comes confidence. You will automatically develop a presence as you
get older, even just a few years older. Shop assistants will
cease to intimidate you when you have money to spend,
and people do have a respect for age. As our experience of
life accumulates, we cease to make the terrible gaffes which

we make in our teens, or perhaps we just cease to care as much.

Most young people seem to have to conform to young people's norms of dress and action: it's part of being young. As you get older you can become eccentric if you wish, and no one will mind. Getting older has its advantages, but it is important that you make the most of any opportunities which present themselves. You have to make the best of your life now, knowing that if you can get things right now your future will be enjoyable. It would be a great mistake to sit back waiting for things to improve, watching life pass you by.

Probably the most rewarding things in life are our personal relationships. You can sacrifice a great deal for the satisfaction of having someone to love, and of having someone love you.

Life is full of great richness, of great emotional and possibly spiritual experiences, and of the joy of love and perhaps parenthood, things that young people think they know about but really can only guess at if they have not had these experiences themselves. Shy people do have the ability to participate in these experiences, even if they start late in life. It's never too late. If you have an open mind and an open heart there is room for great fulfilment. In the course of this book we have been simply opening a door, no more and no less. If you can prise that door open even a little, life's richness will flood in.

Loneliness at any age is a dreadful thing, but loneliness isn't permanent. It only takes one person to put an end to your loneliness, and that person can come from nowhere. This is the incentive to get things moving. If you keep the shutters closed there is no way that the light can come in. You have to at least be willing to let life happen to you, but you can do better, you can go out and live life, push your shyness out of the way and simply get on with it. You can do this—everyone can to a greater or lesser extent. Don't live a life limited by shyness. You don't have to. Quite simply: **Don't Be Shy!**

Index